THE SEVENTH GRADE

Reinhold Messner

THE SEVENTH GRADE

Most extreme climbing

OXFORD UNIVERSITY PRESS
NEW YORK

First published in the U.S.A.
by Oxford University Press
New York
1974

Library of Congress Catalogue Card Number
73–92317

Printed in Great Britain by
Fletcher & Son Ltd, Norwich

Contents

The narratives are interspersed with chapters in which the author delineates his thoughts, preparations and training for the climb which he then describes. These chapters are characterised by the following symbol:

Publisher's Note

Throughout the book, Italian – as opposed to German – names have been used for the mountains in the Dolomites since these are common usage among English-speaking climbers. The author is a South Tyrolean; though of Italian nationality, he is of German ethnic origin and would himself use the German names.

The height of peaks and length of routes, etc., are given in metres, partly because this is how they appear in the author's German original, and also because it is becoming increasingly common in the English-speaking world to use metric terms. Readers may, however, find it helpful to consult the approximate conversion table given below.

1 metre	= 3·28 feet
100 metres	= 328·00 feet
1000 metres	= 3281·00 feet
2000 metres	= 6562·00 feet
3000 metres	= 9843·00 feet
4000 metres	= 13124·00 feet
5000 metres	= 16404·00 feet

KEY

1. Little Dolomites
2. Burél (Schiara Group)
3. Sella Towers
4. Les Droites
5. Mont Blanc
6. Grandes Jorasses
7. Pointes du Domino
8. Eiger
9. Civetta
10. Sassolungo
11. Crozzon di Brenta
12. Castelletto Inferiore
13. Cinque Torri
14. Coronelle
15. Marmolata
16. Monte Cavallo
17. Roda di Vael
18. Furchetta
19. Kaisergebirge
20. Lienz Dolomites

L.Co

Basle

Zurich

SWITZERLAND

Berne

Rhine

L.Geneva

Geneva

Rnone

FRANCE

Chamonix

Isère

Grenoble

Dora Baltea

ITALY

Milan

Turin

Durance

Photographs

Peter Habeler, Heini Holzer, Erich Lackner, Sepp Mayerl, Carlo Mauri, Reinhold Messner, Jürgen Winkler, German Himalayan Foundation of the German Alpine Club.

The Sixth Grade

Definitions and Quotations by Well-known Climbers

In my opinion, the leader of a rope should overcome only such difficulties and hazards (always excepting objective hazards such as crevasses, etc.) as he would meet with as a solo climber.

Paul Preuss, *Künstliche Hilfsmittel auf
Hochtouren*, Deutsche Alpenzeitung
XI. Jg. 1. 1911

For the modern climber, the expression 'Sixth Grade' is equivalent to 'very severe'. The 'tiger', master of his art, on the other hand, regards the first expression as clearer, more comprehensive and expressive than the second. Faint-hearted climbers, and those who prefer to look at a mountain from below, find the expression 'Sixth Grade' something of a mystery, whereas the expression 'very severe' can be clearly understood, although it remains a relative concept, as everyone will define the extreme limit of difficulty in his own way.

Domenico Rudatis, *Das Letzte im Fels*,
Munich 1936

The classification of a climb, and with it the determination of the sixth grade, is made up of the comprehensive consideration of the technical difficulties of each pitch, the steepness, the exposure, the length and to a certain extent the difficulty of route-finding.

Domenico Rudatis, *Das Letzte im Fels*,
Munich 1936

Nobody is capable of accurately determining a sixth grade unless he has knowledge of other sixth grade climbs, which have been positively defined as such by other mountaineers and which he has repeated himself under the same conditions.

Domenico Rudatis, *Das Letzte im Fels*,
Munich 1936

It is no accident that a scale of six grades of difficulty has evolved. It is a natural means of evaluating relative importance. He who surpasses it flouts clear reason, whereas he who falls short of five grades leaves something to be desired.

O W Steiner, *Die Schwierigkeitsbewertung von Bergfahrten*, Vienna 1962

Will the ultimate limit ever be exceeded? It may be that miracles of natural talent under conditions of maximum effort may amplify it somewhat but not by much. The latest first-class achievements since the Solleder-Lettenbauer Route on the Civetta are excursions on the brink of the absolute limit of the possible.

Domenico Rudatis, *Das Letzte im Fels*,
Munich 1936

The absolute technical limit of difficulty in climbing was reached long ago.

O W Steiner, *Die Schwierigkeitsbetertung von Bergfahrten*, Vienna 1962

When the incomparable Paul Preuss wrote: 'Climbers should not only be equal to the climbs they undertake, they should be superior to them', this was stating only a partial truth. It is quite clear that the climber can no longer maintain a superiority over and above the present-day records of the sixth grade; at best one can only surpass them by great skill and luck.

O W Steiner, *Die Schwierigkeitsbewertung von Bergfahrten*, Vienna 1962

Hans Dülfer expressed the opinion that the climbing capacity of the mountaineer can be increased, but that if technical knowledge is to be brought into relationship with the mountain, then fresh scales of difficulty must not be introduced, as the difficulties remain constant. If the climbing capacity increases, the scale of difficulty of the climb correspondingly decreases. If the physical capacity of the climber is equal to the degree of exposure, the lack of stances – in short, the complexity of the climb – then the difficulty remains constant.

O W Steiner

Free climbing on a VI route – the absolute limit of the physically possible – is only suitable for climbers who command a good technique, strength, courage and endurance.

From *Wände, Grate, Gipfel*, Munich 1970

New grades of difficulty cannot be devised just for the purpose of satisfying an unjustifiable alpine ambition.

O W Steiner, *Die Schwierigkeitsbewertung von Bergfahrten*, Vienna 1962

All climbs which as a rule cannot be accomplished without the use of technical aids belong to the 'very severe' sixth grade. The use of adventitious aids is usually compulsory.

Willo Welzenbach

The fact that today many 'extreme' climbers prefer the indiscriminate use of pitons to difficult free rock climbs is partly attributable to our good old Welzenbach Scale and the insidious sixth grade.
Why?
Because VI, the highest grade of difficulty, was assigned to overhanging routes only climbable by artificial means. In this manner, during the fifties, youthful ambition was directed into this blind alley. The preference for over-use of pitons may perhaps decrease, if such

climbs are designated by an 'a' and if pitches of really free climbing of
extreme severity are labelled VI.

Manfred Sturm, Tätigkeitsbericht 1969/70 of
the Safety Committee of the DAV, Munich
1971

The sixth grade is not a dead figure wherein the living voice of the
mountain expired, as many have mistakenly assumed when they con-
sidered the one-sided grading value of isolated pitches. It is, on the
contrary, quite clear that entry into the region of the sixth grade is not
dependent upon the presence of an overhang which has to be worked
upon with piton and rope, or a more or less smooth wall festooned with
ironmongery.

Domenico Rudatis, *Das Letzte im Fels*,
Munich 1936

Grade VI, very severe, partly implies the increased use of artificial
aids, a union of elaborate climbing and piton technique.

O Eidenschink, *Richtiges Bergsteigen*,
Munich 1959

Descriptions of ascents must clearly differentiate between free and
artificial climbing. A whole route or isolated pitches are climbed 'free'
when pitons, rope slings or other aids are employed as belays and not
as a means of progression, i.e. as artificial footholds. This means that
if pitons are used as holds or étriers are employed on a route designated
as a free climb, then this route is reduced in status to that of an A
grade. The valuation of difficulties in free climbing is indicated by
Roman figures from I to VI, with intermediate stages or lower $(-)$
and upper $(+)$ *limits.*

The grading of difficulty in artificial climbing is indicated by the
letter A with the addition of numerals from 0 to 4. Where expansion
bolts are used, this is indicated by the addition of a small e, e.g. A2e.

Six grades are sufficient to denote the difficulties involved in free
climbing. Free climbing of a pitch of VI is reserved for exceptional

climbers. It might here be stressed that maximum effort and skill lie only within the scope of free climbing and have nothing to do with artificial methods.

UIAA Safety Commission under
Fritz Wiessner, 1971

The use of technical aids and belays, compared to free climbing, always degrades the difficulties of a route to a greater or less degree. The grade of a climb, especially the sixth grade, always takes into account this reduction of status.

Domenico Rudatis, *Das Letzte im Fels*,
Munich 1936

Grade VI implies unusual difficulties and is only for the élite. Minimum hand and footholds demand exceptionally strong fingers, and entail great exposure and minimal stances. Where artificial climbing is resorted to, there will be considerable use of pitons, karabiners and étriers. When climbing free, VI+ denotes a pitch approaching the falling-off zone and should only be attempted by climbers at the top of their form, under favourable conditions (dry rock), taking maximum advantage of the nature of the rock (hand and foot holds, friction) and use of up-to-date equipment (such as modern boots with vibram soles). A Grade VI+ climb is impossible in winter without the use of additional pitons as a means of progression. Experience has shown that a climb of this type only attains its maximum difficulty when no additional pitons can be positioned, in other words, when the nature of the rock does not permit the pitch to be climbed artificially.

Werner Munter

In view of the fact that man has reached the uttermost limit of technical difficulties, anything higher lies beyond the bounds of human endeavour.

O W Steiner, *Die Schwierigkeitsbewertung von Bergfahrten*, Vienna 1962

Climbing a crack on the Salathé Wall on El Capitan, Yosemite. 'Some of their routes measure up to our extremely severe free climbing routes,' said Peter Habeler, who was one of the first Europeans to climb this magnificent route.

The Seventh Grade

Tendencies and Standards in Contemporary
Non-competitive Mountaineering

There are two tendencies which are clearly differentiated in contemporary extreme mountaineering: the search for new, difficult direct ascents and the striving after still greater difficulties in the Alps, in Yosemite, in the Pyrenees . . .

At the beginning of 1950, climbs such as the Gabriel-Livanos Route on Cima Su Alto in the Civetta and the West Face of the Dru in the Western Alps were accomplished with the increased use of artificial aids, where formerly leading climbers employing the traditional methods had failed. This development proceeded apace and at the end of the fifties would seem to have surpassed itself by such climbs as the Brandler-Hasse Route on the North Face of the Cima Grande and the French Route on the Cima Ovest.

As technique improved, difficulties of every sort were overcome and every alpine face was conquered; the extreme climbers or at least some of them became non-competitive.

Non-competitive climbing – in contrast to mountaineering for the sake of conquest – seeks out difficulties in order to solve them in a distinctive manner. The climber subjects himself to predetermined rules which are very important to him – perhaps even for the development of alpine mountaineering.

Non-competitive mountaineering is not a phenomenon of the present day, it is not related to any particular period of time; it has appealed to individual climbers for more than a hundred years.

Alfred Frederick Mummery became a non-competitive climber when he learned to do without guides and accomplished the difficult climbs of his times on his own. Paul Preuss refused to use pitons, yet nevertheless was able to overcome the most difficult climbs of his day without their aid. Later on, other climbers, Hias Rebitsch and Walter Bonatti in particular (the latter frequently climbing solo and employing a limited amount of artificial aids), stood out for 'fair play' and, in spite of this, led the way in routes of the utmost difficulty. In the summer of 1971 Enzo Cozzolino, a determined opponent of the expansion bolt, climbed a dozen or so routes using normal pitons, where leading climbers before him had failed even when using a chisel.

It is interesting to reflect that Mummery introduced the fifth grade in the existing Alpine Scale and that, with Preuss, the sixth grade saw the light of day, and it would not be too presumptuous to infer that Bonatti and Cozzolino have introduced the seventh grade.

The foremost climbers in the United States have for years endeavoured to make the first free ascents of the old and partly technical routes and in some cases have succeeded in doing so. A route of the highest scale of difficulty, where some fifty pitons were used as a means of progression (i.e. as holds), must obviously be much higher in the scale if these pitons were removed. If the most difficult routes in the Alps can be climbed solo and often without any form of belay, then it stands to reason that a roped party can cope with greater difficulties than those hitherto encountered. From the fact that routes of the sixth grade can be climbed in winter in cold and snowy conditions without artificial aids, I deduce that the possibilities of free climbing in more favourable conditions are not yet completely exhausted.

When the sixth grade was introduced about fifty years ago as the ultimate endeavour, it did not mean that this limit could not be surpassed. Rigid adherence to the six grades of difficulty resulted in the routes being demoted every ten years and the sixth grade of difficulty becoming a synonym for a series of extremely

The Cerro Torre in Patagonia. On the right, climbing the unconquered
West Face. After Cesare Maestri's ascent in 1971 with the aid of
a drill, it lost something of its charm. Perhaps it might provide
an incentive for the seventh grade.

difficult ascents, which actually reduced to two grades. If one undertakes a modern sixth grade climb bearing in mind the nomenclature AO, that is to say that the climbing is free and any existing piton is used neither as a hand- nor foot-hold, the following ridiculous situation arises: the Via de Ideale (Aste/Solina) (VI) on the Marmolata d'Ombretta is half a grade higher than the Philipp-Flamm Route on the Civetta (VI), the North-West Face Direct on the Second Sella Tower (VI+) is a grade more difficult than the Tissi Route on the First Tower (V–VI); the Pilastrodi Rozes (VI +) is easier than the Central Pillar on the Monte Cavallo (VI) and several of the Goedecke Routes (VI or VI—) are without doubt two grades less than the South Face Direct on the Marmolata di Rocca (VI).

This chaotic state of affairs in the upper difficulty bracket will get worse as the years go by unless the scale of difficulty is allowed to remain open at the top.

The scale of difficulty involving six grades has interested me for a long time. The figures are self-evident but the designation of words such as 'very difficult', 'severe' and 'very severe' is confusing. While generally satisfied with the lay-out of the scale, I am not happy about the upper range. This is probably due to the old definition of the sixth grade: VI being the absolute limit of potential climbing. One might as well say that after the ten seconds run of Armin Hary, 'This is the fastest time which will ever be run, therefore it is no use counting any time below this.'

Naturally progress becomes slower the more we approach the maximum, but it is there and should not *a priori* be excluded.

For this reason I would never regard the sixth grade as the limit of human possibility in mountain climbing. And even if it were so defined, it would not actually exist as such. There would be no route of the sixth grade, as nobody could prove that they had reached the limit of human capacity. A climber can only attain the limit of his own personal physical capacity and will go on trying to keep this up, even when during the passage of time it eludes him.

By means of exertion and concentration the climber keeps alert, he sees things in a new light with a clarity and spiritual mobility which can for example be attained by meditation. Above all he sees himself in a new relationship to the world.

In accordance with my experience this only teaches the climber to know his own physical limits. That is not to say that such conditions are restricted to extremes: anyone, whether he is at home in the second or the sixth grade, can achieve this experience. A knowledgeable climber must certainly undertake longer and more difficult tours in order to attain the state of spiritually deep strength of vision. The desire to do so will irresistibly drive the level of performance ever higher.

Thoughts of accomplishment and success are always in the foreground and they encourage one to attempt greater and more difficult climbs.

'Success' is equally responsible for the tendency towards non-competitive climbing, as the pleasure in taking part in any activity generally depends upon the success of the venture. Lack of success diminishes the active impulse.

What market price or valuation can one put upon this success when climbing has no end-product? Doubtless in accordance with the scale of difficulty and the importance of the tour. For example, the Walker Spur rates higher than the South Face of the Aiguille du Midi and the South-East Face of the Fleischbank lower than the North Face Direct of the Lalidererspitze.

The meeting of man and mountain has a fixed boundary and this becomes ever more firmly determined. When unlimited technical aids are introduced into climbs of the greatest difficulty, not only does the problem disappear but the limit itself is washed out. For this reason, as technical aids were perfected and became effective, many climbers exercised restraint in order to bring about a proper relationship between man and mountain.

The best young climbers of today have assumed this sporting attitude. They have a quiet laugh about Cesare Maestri's expansion bolts on the Cerro Torre or the 'Brazilian Expedition' of some Tyrolean guides on the Sugarloaf.

Today climbs are no longer valued for their publicity rating but rather for their style and the surmounting of their difficulties. One strives towards an ideal, the ideal of the elegant, most direct and incomparably difficult route.

This ideal is a limit which nobody will ever attain. We can only approach it, rather like the hundred metre runner who will never do it in five seconds, or the pole-vaulter who will never reach ten metres. Nevertheless it would be presumptuous to declare 9·8 seconds or six metres as the limits of possibility. In this, as in other spheres, the scale is left open at the top as a spur towards greater records.

It would be equally presumptuous to set the sixth grade as the extreme limit of free climbing. Naturally we are not dealing here with an exact measurable scale, but only with estimated values. Nevertheless I would venture to maintain that there are climbers who are capable of exceeding the difficulties of today by a few grades.

Although I totally reject a climber's Olympiad, climbing to a time limit or for any awarded marks, in other words, any form of competitive climbing activity, I am still fascinated by the idea of the seventh grade of difficulty.

The scale of difficulty must remain open at the top without an imposed limit. Having attained this, I would venture to ascribe Grade VI or VI+ to climbs and I would be fascinated to see who would be the first to climb a seventh grade route.

My aim in non-competitive climbing would be the striving for greater difficulties combined with a voluntary ban on technical aids. In order to advance in the scale of difficulties, the climber must take a voluntary step backwards as regards the use of artificial methods.

Only by better training, skill and much experience, can the climber be certain of mastering the sixth grade so that he can climb it solo, up and down and under winter conditions. He is so certain of success on climbs of the sixth grade that he will seek out greater difficulties once again to reach his physical limit and the fresh experiences which go with it.

When what American scientists have worked out over the years comes to pass, namely that 'the conception and setting of aims arise in the region of uncertain outlets', when the younger generation of climbers gets round to voluntary renunciation of technical aids and when an open-ended scale of difficulties is brought in, then and only then will the seventh grade reach the Alps.

When this becomes a reality, then climbing will be capable of making a lasting step forward – a step which is in principle boundless.

Suddenly the summer came to an end. I was working again and kept remembering the great routes I had undertaken. Plans which I had formerly thought beyond my reach had become achievements. I had climbed faces which a year ago I would not even have dreamed about. For the most part I had climbed solo and in a style which others whom it did not concern considered apparently foolhardy. I was at the top of my form and it didn't bother me at all. I had the feeling that this summer my life had been positively enriched.

Until one day when someone (actually there were several) decided that it was time that I became aware of my responsibilities. (Thousands die daily of hunger, thousands on the roads and an equal number die from the diseases of our times: heart disease, hardening of the arteries, boredom . . .)

'Apparently,' said some, 'you seek out danger for danger's sake.'

'No,' said I, 'quite the contrary.'

'You climb alone, without any form of belay and often in bad weather; this is a dangerous business which will come to a bad end.'

'It will end badly,' they repeated. I smiled, although I knew very well that by smiling like that I would not make many friends.

'Why don't you admit,' said they with a remarkable lack of sympathetic understanding, 'that you are foolhardy?'

I shook my head. (They had to find some reason for my behaviour and doubtless spoke behind my back of neurosis.)

'Experience shows that you can't get away with it forever – maybe for a month, at the most for a summer.'

'Could be.'

'And you still do it?'

'I feel quite safe, even safer than when there are two.'

'That's just not possible.'

'*I can assess my own qualities, but not those of my mate, and I would rather not sit in judgement on him or send him down.*'

'*As we understand it, you don't belay so as not to endanger your mate?*'

'*I am always well prepared, as I begin my training early in the spring.*'

'*Possibly,*' said they, '*but have you thought what might have happened this summer?*'

'*Obviously nothing happened.*' This infuriated them.

'*Why don't you admit that you were lucky, very lucky?*'

I said nothing, but I saw the stones sweeping down the ice slopes of the North Face of Les Droites that afternoon when I was walking up to the hut. I looked at the stump of the piton hammer left in my hand that day on the Soldà Route on the Sassolungo. I heard the waterfall in the exit couloir of the Philipp-Flamm Route on the Civetta. I saw the falling body of my companion on the Baffelan and thought of those know-alls standing at the foot of the Second Sella Tower and talking about the mountain rescue services.

Many times I have had to hold on good and hard so as not to fall off the face.

An exhibition climb in Padua. The prusik loop did not grip until I cleaned the wooden pole of grease and rubbed fine sand into the surface.

It All Began with a Game

It was on the second day of the *Festa della Matricola*. In the square in front of the Pedrocchi, one of the best cafés in Padua, a crowd of students was watching the battle of the *goliardi* on the *palo della cucagna* (greasy pole). There were probably eight or nine of them, who were keeping the vast crowd on tenterhooks. Shouting, music and loudspeakers – a typical Italian student festival.

The *festa* lasted for three days. The University was closed and we students were on holiday. Roads were closed, the cinemas were full and games and betting proliferated everywhere. One of these games was climbing the *palo della cucagna*, a pole about fifteen metres high, which was set up in the middle of the square in the old town. As the pole was liberally coated with a thick layer of fat, it would seem impossible to climb it, added to which the dirty state of the participants was just nobody's business. For this reason the students, called *goliardi*, wore old military uniforms and were equipped with cloths and fine sand. They attempted with considerable tenacity to swarm up the pole, but all in vain.

The pole had not been climbed for years, so a prize of five thousand lire was offered for the man who could reach the crown at the top. The crown, a rusty bicycle rim, was adorned with all manner of rubbish, sausages, pasta and so on.

Another group of students had a go – shouting, booing, encouragement from the loudspeaker and music. All windows around the square were wide open and everybody was watching. After a few metres the leading man slipped down again and his companions looked on helplessly. He stood at the foot, swore and shook his head, looked angrily up the pole and started again. His companions heaved and pushed behind. Way up the pole a cord was hanging down. He seized it, pulled himself up and put his foot in a loop at the bottom of the cord. As he clung breathlessly to it, the crowd shouted encouragement from below.

However, the cord slid slowly, very slowly, downwards. Two of the climber's friends immediately took up positions at the foot, a third man climbed on their shoulders and, supported by a fourth man, managed to arrest his slow descent. The leader took the weight off the cord and tried to push it upwards and place his foot in the loop. The human pyramid below him wavered, groaned, shouted out loud and finally collapsed.

So far I had only been an observer, but now I realised that they were getting nowhere. Then suddenly the cord, which was hanging about a third of the way up, gave me an idea. I thereupon asked the jury whether it was permissible to use this cord.

'Naturally.'

'And a second one?'

'Well – yes, but no ladders and no nails.'

Such were the rules. So I put my name down for an attempt as all the others had done who thought they had a chance.

'I want to have a go,' said I.

'Alone?'

'Yes, alone.' The students on the jury just laughed.

'Not a hope,' said one. Nevertheless I was determined to try.

'Right, off you go!'

'Half a moment,' I said, 'I'll be back in a second,' and I ran off. Two minutes later I was back – carrying a bag.

I put it down by the pole, opened it and took out some articles of clothing and put them on. I managed to make one of the bystanders understand that I wanted his old uniform. He gave it to me and I put it on over my own clothing. I then filled the pockets with fine sand and some pieces of foam rubber which were spread out at the foot of the pole in case of a fall. I now looked fat and bulging.

I wrapped a cord twice round the pole, pushed it as far as it would go and pulled on it. It held. I knotted the free end into a loop and stepped into it. I swung backwards and forwards and then straightened up. With one hand I loosened the loop which the others had left dangling and with the other hand I grasped the pole firmly. I now managed to wind the second loop twice round the pole and put my other foot in it.

I now pushed the loops alternately up the pole and rapidly gained height. As I pulled on one loop, I took the weight off the other one and pushed it up a bit further. All those who up to this time had been laughing now stared in astonishment. Silence reigned over the square. I cleaned off the fat with foam rubber, rubbed in some sand and pushed the loop higher up. Step by step I made slow progress.

Two hours later I was nearly there. The crown moved slowly backwards and forwards – forwards and backwards. When my sand ran out my South Tyrol friends threw me up a small bagful. The crowd roared and the people in the windows applauded.

A moment later I pulled myself up to the crown. The town went mad. The sound waves surged up to the walls of the houses round the square, were thrown back and engulfed me. With an exuberant gesture I threw the bits and pieces hanging from the crown down to the crowd below: pasta, two plucked chickens, sausages . . .

Everybody was pushing and shoving in the square, hands waved in the air. The noise increased to a wild crescendo of enthusiasm as I untied one of the loops and threw it down into the square. It was no more use to me; however, they fought over it. In the meantime I climbed out of the second loop, left it hanging and slid down the pole.

I had hardly reached the ground before I was overwhelmed. They shook my hand, clapped me on the back . . . photos were taken . . . Italian ecstasy.

The *palo* had been climbed again and solo at that! I never had a reception after any of my climbs like the one I had after this spectacular ascent. 'Using a prusik loop just made it child's play,'

I said and pressed forward to the jury to receive my prize. Five thousand lire! I was invited into the Pedrocchi and while I was being fêted, I had a quiet laugh to myself, thinking how easy it was to acquire a measure of admiration from a few students.

As I returned to my lectures, which had restarted, the square was empty. Respectable citizens were annoyed about the pasta on the ground and a street cleaner was starting to clean up the paper and other rubbish which littered the square.

As I turned round the corner to the Piazza Cavour, I looked back to the *palo* standing forlorn and unnoticed in the square. One of my loops hung right at the top. 'Just as if someone wanted to hang himself,' I thought as I entered the lecture hall just as the professor began explaining the hexagonal system.

I now began my training in Padua for my climbs in the summer. I got up earlier than usual and ran a few laps round the quadrangle of the students' quarters. I increased the number day by day. At weekends I drove over to the practice rocks at Teolo, where I usually met Italian friends.

Every town with alpine traditions has its own practice area. Munich climbers train in the Isar Valley, the Viennese on the Rax, Paris has its Fontainebleau rocks and the Innsbruck men practise in the Hottinger quarry. The Padua climbers favour the Rocca Pendice as their practice ground. The rocks, which are of the conglomerate type, are about 120 metres high and only five minutes outside the town. Moss adheres to the slabs on the lesser-used routes and the pitons are eaten away by rust. Bushes grow here and there, and just below the top there are some small trees which serve as belays.

The shortest routes are the most popular; they are clean, the pitons are cemented in and the holds are polished with much use. Most of the Padua climbers know every ledge and crack, and climb up and down them like squirrels.

As in every other training area, the Rocca Pendice has its 'boulder' where novices are tried out. When they asked me to climb this fifteen metre traverse on overhanging rocks, I felt that my 'mountaineering honour' was involved. I took a good look at it, rubbed my fingers with chalk to keep them dry and tried to breathe slowly and regularly. I started off, traversed from left to right and back again. When I had finished I felt that in the eyes of the Padua men I had done my stuff.

This was the beginning of a great summer, but I did not know it as yet. What I had in mind was to pass all my exams at the University and leave my climbing until later.

For six months I had forced myself to hurry from lecture hall to lecture hall, from the Common Room to some institute or other and back to my room. Nobody forbade me from going to the mountains, yet I resisted the call.

Everything went awry however. I hadn't planned it this way and I still don't know whether I would have made a different decision if I had to choose again.

The North-West Face of the Civetta. The notorious Philipp-Flamm Route, on the demarcation line between light and shade, is one of the most difficult routes in the Alps.

A Sunday Near the City

I stood by my desk in an unsettled frame of mind. It was Sunday and my books lay open before me.

The morning mist, which usually descends over Padua during the first weeks of spring, had dispersed. The sun was shining outside. I looked out over the houses: Institute, lecture halls, laboratories, etc. Trees stood in the quadrangle outside my window. I leaned out of the window and looked down the street. The air between the houses was full of exhaust fumes. My head seemed full of the subdued noise which rose from the streets. From time to time a few passers-by hurried along the pavements towards the centre of the city. I felt nauseated with the town and turned back into the room.

Suddenly I heard the cries of children; apparently they were going on an outing into the country with their parents and they were expressing their delight. I guessed as much and suddenly I was overcome with the desire to do likewise.

They got out at Teolo and joined other children playing on the grassy slopes leading up to the Rocca Pendice. They shouted and ran about and dogs barked. Far above them where the rocks appeared over the bushes, I saw some grown-ups climbing. The noise of the pitons being driven into the rocks drifted down to us.

I sat down on a rock and watched the children playing. They had tied a rope onto a board and were dragging it uphill. When they reached the top they sat on it and slid down the slope shouting with joy. A dog ran alongside them. They steered the thing with their feet between the bushes and stones. The children were enjoying it as much as the dog. Only the grown-ups looked a trifle dubious abut the green stains on their clothes.

Before long I went back to the car, put on a pullover and my climbing trousers, changed my shoes and wandered over to the 'Grotto' and started climbing. The Grotto was a training area, full of holes and cracks, about four metres high. It was excellent for practice as the rocks were overhanging and as they were so low one could climb to the limit of falling off.

Giorgio broke away from the group of children and sauntered over to me. He was chewing a piece of grass as I was traversing the convex wall and, leaning against an oak tree, followed my every movement. 'Alpinista?' he enquired. I shook my head.

He then tried his hand at the Grotto, but scarcely got off the ground. This was not surprising as he could not have been more than twelve years old. He told me later that his father was a first-rate climber and had given him mountaineering books to read. He already knew what a piton was but did not understand how one drove them in. I explained and knocked one or two into cracks for his benefit. He told me all about the climbs his father had done.

In Giorgio's opinion only a genius was capable of mastering a sixth grade climb. Although I would like to have told him that any well-trained healthy climber was capable of this, I refrained from doing so as I did not wish to denigrate his hero.

Having now got thoroughly warmed-up, I said goodbye to Giorgio and went over to the North Face of the Rocca Pendice. It is about 180 metres high and the classical climb on it is the Via Carrugati. It is also the most popular. It had been cleaned of grass, all the pitons held and it was climbed at least five times every Sunday in the spring.

Two ropes were just about to start this fourth and fifth grade climb. I knew it well and decided to watch them.

Their movements were sedate as they tied on and tested the knots. The second man carefully laid the rope over his shoulder and held it in his hands. The leader went to the foot of the climb – a quick look at the equipment, the piton hammer in the right

Reinhold Messner on the 'practice boulder'. After a lecture in Carrara, the organisers challenged him to climb this jam crack, wearing a lounge suit and white shirt!

position, then a nod to his companion.

The first few steps were a bit clumsy. He inserted a piton and, after climbing up a few metres, he threw the rope over a projection and straddled across a wide groove, looking stylish and rhythmical. It was then that I recognised him – he was Giorgio's father.

Everything was just like a great mountain climb, only the tension was missing. Something is absent on a practice climb in a training area. There is the start and the rope run-outs to the top, but the real adventure begins with the solitude; when he has achieved this, the climber finds himself in another world.

I put all my equipment under a boulder and climbed after them. After a few minutes I had overtaken both parties. My pace increased with each metre and I felt myself getting stronger as I went on. When I reached the top I was no more tired than when I started.

I descended by the normal route on the south side, ran round the whole massif and climbed up the north face of the next rock. The other two parties were in the middle of the face when I reached them and before they had overcome the small rock roof, the key point of the climb, I was already at the summit. This second route was shorter than the first, about 120 metres, so in all I had climbed about 300 metres.

There are those who may say that I had only one object in all this rapid climbing, namely to please myself and satisfy my own ego. But they would be wrong, for my principal object was to climb at least 500 metres without a rest, as the Dolomite faces are about that long. I wanted to put myself to the test before I went to the mountains again – in the middle of a great face it might be too late. I climbed another two routes that afternoon, in the course of which I met the two parties from the Via Carrugati. They were visibly annoyed by my speed and seemed to consider it foolhardy. When one of my friends told me this over a cup of coffee in the old town a few days later, I just smiled but could not help thinking that one is much more prone to get angry with oneself than with the training methods of others!

I increased my morning runs to an hour. A few students joined me and sometimes we ran for a wager.

I quite got to like these morning runs and in my opinion they are the best way of getting into condition, and I would especially recommend them to ice climbers. Endurance is a major part of the basic preparation for them as it is with rock climbers – if one hasn't got it, better remain in the practice area.

In order to exercise my fingers, I did a hanging traverse along a beading on the wall of the students' quarters, once each way, making sixty metres in all. This was good for developing the muscles of the forearms.

There was no longer any snow on the lower south-facing slopes of the Alps. Claudio Cima, a student from Milan, had invited me to participate in an excursion to the Piccole Dolomite. These mountains stand on the fringe of the Alps between Vicenza and Trieste. They are not really mountains in the true sense of the word, neither are they a practice area, but something in between. In the spring when snow makes access to the main Dolomite faces difficult, they are very popular. Here there are walls 200 or 300 metres high, vertical, brittle and difficult. Climbers of such repute as Soldà and Carlesso learned their first steps in mountaineering on these walls.

The disintegrated rock demands clean climbing and careful treatment of the holds. Due to the steepness, the eye learns to accustom itself to the exposure and the finger tips are hardened by the rough limestone surface and the damp grass. This did not matter much to us, the important thing was that we were on the way again.

Encounter at the Station

The chestnut blossom was still young and fresh. I was standing by my car in the shade of the trees reading Claudio's last letter. We did not know each other, we were only pen-friends. Months ago he had hinted that a joint mountaineering expedition might be on the cards and that we could talk about it later. In due course we fixed up this weekend.

Passengers were streaming out of the station, carrying bags. They came from Milan, Turin and the wide Po Valley and they were all in a hurry. Outside in the brilliant sunshine on the paved square they hailed taxis or disappeared down side streets.

'Hallo, Reinhold,' said a voice behind me. 'Have you been waiting long?'

It was Claudio. He didn't look a bit like a climber, whitefaced and dressed in jeans like all the other youngsters. I was also pale after nine months of classes.

On the way up to the hut we began to get sunburnt. We became aware of this next afternoon on the South Ridge of the Piccolo Apostolo. In the morning we repeated the classical Soldà Route on the Baffelan, an enormous system of dièdres and couloirs, partly streaming with melting snow. Here, on the sharp arête, the rock was dry and the grass on the stances yellow and burned by the sun. High above our heads an overhang leaned outwards; it seemed friendly and warm in the rays of the setting sun. The route led upwards along either side of the ridge like a ladder.

The green of the plains faded away in the distance into the blue of the horizon. A little smoke from the hut below curled upwards into the still air.

The next stop was the summit. The snow glistened on the north faces, thick and hard as ice. Here the ground was damp, not yet frozen. The nights will soon be cold, I thought.

Next day we were climbing on the upper part of the Carlesso Route on the Baffelan – or so we thought. Actually we had strayed off the proper route and were on the very severe Soldà Pillar. The last rope-length was difficult and the rock unsound. There were no pitons to be seen – sixth grade. A stance was clearly visible on a pocket of turf. Sure enough, there was an old piton behind a firm piece of rock. It was waist-high and seemed firm enough, so I attached a rope sling to it. To make doubly sure I inserted another piton.

It is a habit of mine to drive in two pitons at a stance, so I inserted a medium Cassin piton in a hole in the rock just above my head and tied myself firmly on by means of a figure-of-eight knot. Now I was happy, Claudio could come on up. He was soon by my side and as the terrain above us did not look too difficult, he led through. A large ring piton in a groove to the right attracted his attention. I advised him to tie off onto this piton which was sticking out about ten centimetres from the rock. He tied a line with a simple prusik loop round the blade of the piton and attached the rope to the loop by means of a karabiner. Ten metres further on the groove petered out into the vertical edge of the Pillar. Here he found a piton which he clipped into and went on climbing.

It must have been very difficult. He drove in another piton and vanished behind the ridge. I sensed danger and paid more attention than usual.

Suddenly there was a rattle of pitons, a jerk (the first piton must have come out, I thought), followed by another jerk. I was pulled off my stance and then the tension eased. (Good, I thought, the second piton must have held.) Suddenly, without warning, I was pulled upwards about two metres.

When everything had quietened down, I realised the danger of our situation. Claudio was hanging about ten metres below me. The old piton at the stance had been jerked out and upwards by the sudden pull. The second piton had also gone and we were now dependent upon the old ring piton and the Cassin piton, which I had inserted as a precautionary measure at the stance. Although I was in a tricky situation I managed to fix the rope and get Claudio up. It was only then that I realised that my hands were burned by the rope.

We abseiled down and went back to the hut. It was full, so we said nothing. At last, when they had all gone, we were alone with the guardian and told him our story. Fortunately neither of us had serious injuries but we had had enough and only wanted to descend the valley.

On the way down we met Gino Soldà. He was sitting on a wooden bench at the side of the path and he told us about his golden days. 'Extreme climbing was not suitably recognised in the old days,' he complained. 'It was quite different then, not at all like today. Our first ascents were made under great difficulty, with many setbacks and humiliations.' When I revealed to him that I already knew his route on the Piz de Ciavàzes and that I liked his route on the Langkofel, he only smiled. Six months later I wrote to Claudio that I had climbed it solo. He was studying in New York and his answering letter seemed depressed.

'This city is so cold' – and he didn't only mean the frost – 'the worst is being alone among so many people. I often think of our climbing days . . . there was so much sunshine then.'

The following weekend in the practice area, I was in good form; the summer lay ahead and was full of promise. To be sure, my coming exams did much to curb my bumptiousness but caution also played a part. Nevertheless, I carried on with my training day in and day out before I made up my mind to attempt a solo climb in the Schiara Group.

These mountains in the southern region of the Dolomites are situated in very desolate terrain. Deeply wooded gorges lead up from the valley bottom at Belluno and Cordevole to the unusually light-coloured rocks, which here and there are overgrown with grass. There are some enterprising routes on the more important peaks and high above the Val di Piero, completely concealed, lies one of the greatest of the very severe Dolomite faces, the South-West Face of the Burél. Konrad Renzler and I were able to make the second ascent of this route. On the way up to the climb I thought that I had discovered a possible new route on the South-West Face, but later on I found that it had already been done by Richard Goedecke. I found a sketch in the current number of Alpinismus, *which I cut out and stuck in my pocket on the morning of 17 May before I left Padua by car.*

Just How Hard is Difficult?

First Solo Ascent of the South Face of the Burél

For two hours I had been driving towards Belluno. For the first time this spring I had a definite object in view and had adopted a plan to accomplish it. As the plan had been worked out to the last detail, it did not seem to me to be over-ambitious and, because I was as well prepared as possible, it had to succeed. Above all, I thought, I must take it slowly to the foot of the climb so as not to overtire myself.

As soon as I reached the hut I changed my clothes. Apart from the guardian, the hut was empty. At this time of year the mountain ramblers of Belluno were roaming in the lower valleys. I fastened a rope on my back and tied a bundle of pitons to my harness. This did not take long, I had done it so often before. Having stuffed a torch, an anorak and a handful of dried fruit into my pockets, I left the hut.

I walked up the narrow path to the gap, dangling my crash helmet. When I arrived at the foot of the wall, I was no longer sure of my whereabouts as there was no cairn. This provided a further reason to examine the face more closely. A grey solid rock rib led upwards to a yellow belt of rocks topped by horizontal overhangs.

I delicately balanced up the first steep pitches, alone and without a belay. I had no fear of falling off as all my movements were always well thought out and if I ran into trouble I came down again. However, this rarely happened.

The holds, eroded by water, were rough to the touch, but the rock was not as compact as, for example, the Civetta or the Tre

Cima. I was fully aware of the fact that, come what may, I must at all costs take care that my strength did not give out before I was clear of the overhangs.

The wall fell away clear a hundred metres below me. I climbed more carefully and slowly and arrived at the crux just to the right of the second roof. This crux consisted of an almost holdless overhang, below which was an expansion bolt.

I massaged my forearms as I anticipated a pitch of the sixth grade, if not actually on the overhang, then higher up. It is not good to linger too long in such a place. However, I always have a little reserve strength left in my fingers and I can even climb if suffering from cramp. But this strength is soon used up if one is wrestling with an overhang and cannot retreat. Anyone trapped in such a situation will eventually come off, not perhaps at once, but soon. He would fall off so suddenly that he would only have time for a cry and yet so slowly that he could push himself off the wall and his whole life would flash through his brain.

I did not know this from my own experience but from others, as I had never fallen off when leading. The air was pleasantly warm and my hands were well placed on the rock. I thought back to the cloudless days of October last year when we almost died of thirst on the South Face – two days in the hot sun and only diluted fruit juice to drink. Today, however, I had nothing to drink but was not thirsty.

Just below the overhang I toyed with the idea of retreating, but I carried on and did not consider it again.

While taking a breather on my stance, I observed blades of grass falling in the shafts of sunlight. It must be windy on top. I pulled in the rope behind me; the climbing was easier now. Up as far as a shelf on the upper part of the face, I often changed direction. I climbed to the left and to the right but always upwards. Often the wall eased off a bit so that I thought the summit was near, although I had carefully studied the route beforehand.

Sometimes I was no longer certain of the way ahead; either there were two equally difficult possibilities or I had lost the way. But I got back on the right course. That sounds as though I was particularly astute, but a sense of direction is one of the instincts of a mountaineer.

I do not hold myself up to be a hero. I was very cautious, perhaps overcautious. I only do what I see and sometimes even less than that. The route on the South Face of the Burél was certainly not as difficult as I had expected.

Suddenly I noticed that the terrain was becoming indistinct. I was shrouded in mist. This mist was not welling up from the depths, it was in the air. I pulled myself together and went on. On the top I looked over the summit rocks for the way down but the mist was just as thick on the other side.

I was just able to see gullies and couloirs dropping away below me. Each gully looked like the next. I climbed down one which was full of snow and it led to the foot of the wall. I ran back to the hut as quickly as I could. When I got there, the mist had thinned a little.

As I was picking up my rucksack outside the hut, the guardian tapped me on the shoulder. 'Is the South Face more difficult than the South-West Face?' he asked.

'What do you mean?' I said and laughed.

I had made the mistake of expecting the climb to be like its description in the hut book and in periodicals – a climb of the sixth grade. I said goodbye and stumbled down the uneven track, sensing thoughtful stares behind me, but I did not turn round.

TELEGRAMMA URGENTE

8 20 MAG 20 II 52 URGENT 6 351CC 25. OEAV +

| Modulario C - Tel. 65 |
| Mod. 30-A Ug. - Ediz. 1968 |

INDICAZIONI D'URGENZA	Ricevuto il			Le ore si contano sul meridiano corrispondente al tempo medio dell'Europa Centrale. Nei telegrammi impressi a caratteri romani, il primo numero dopo il nome del luogo di origine rappresenta quello del telegramma, il secondo quello delle parole, gli altri la data, l'ora e i minuti della presentazione.		Bollo d'ufficio
U G	Pel circuito N.			
Qualifica	DESTINAZIONE	PROVENIENZA	NUM.	PAROLE	DATA DELLA PRESENTAZIONE		Via e indicazioni eventuali d'ufficio
					Giorno e mese	Ore e minuti	

51D INNSBCK A 1126 URGENT INNSBRUCK TEL 810 28 20 1105 =

HAETTEN DICH FUER UNSERE ANDENEXPEDITION BENOETIGT AUSRUESTUNG

VORHANDEN ABFLUG 25. MAI BITTE TELEGRAFIERE SOFORT ZURUECK =

OEAV WIEDMANN +

Would like you for Andes Expedition. Equipment available.
Flight 25 May. Please wire at once.

OEAV Wiedmann

This wire from Innsbruck upset all my plans for study. Five days later I was flying to Rio de Janeiro. In the meantime I had got my passport, had all the necessary injections and purchased extra equipment. On the way to Venice I dozed off in the car and went off the road. In spite of this, I arrived at the Peruvian consulate on time and obtained the visas for Lima.

Despite my advanced training, I was not sufficiently in condition for such a great expedition. As I did not get my invitation until just before departure, there was nothing else I could do about it, except refuse. However the approach march and, above all, the climbing at

6000 metres above sea level put me in cracking form, which I had never experienced before.

For more than a month we proceeded on foot and, together with Peter Habeler, I succeeded in climbing the North-East Face of the Yerupaya Grande (6634m) and the South-West Face of the Yerupaya Chico (6121m). Climbing in the thin air and carrying a heavy rucksack had a more positive effect on my body than any training. I particularly noticed this on the way back and every day I did a cross-country run so as to maintain my physical condition. I used to run on my toes in order to strengthen the calves. Occasionally I would step up the pace until my heart and lungs were strained to the uttermost.

Back in Lima I weighed 155 pounds, twenty-five pounds less than when I set out and my state of health was excellent. I had no idea that in Italy they thought I was dead.

On my return from South America, I stayed at home for some days to deal with my mail and sort out my equipment. I kept my fingers in form by doing a daily traverse on the crumbling wall of an old saw mill.

The thin air of the 6000 metre peaks and my loss of weight had made me so fit that I wanted to climb more than ever. The following Sunday I went up to the Sella Pass and climbed around the Towers there. Quite by chance I met some students from Padua who were watching a party on the North Ridge of the Second Sella Tower. For some time they just could not take it in that it really was I who was talking to them, although we had been studying together a few months ago. They also had thought that I was dead, as they told me later on. This took place on the Sella Pass, at midday in the middle of July.

Celebration of my Resurrection

'You're mad,' said the old man. A few minutes ago I had returned from the dead and now I was mad. Just plain mad.

'I've never seen anything like it,' he went on, pointing to my long yellow corduroy trousers, which although quite new were worn at the knees. I had bought them for the Andes Expedition but hardly wore them as it was too cold for them at Base Camp.

'I've been around in the Alps for years, but never, no never, have I seen anything like them. You're mad!' Up to now, that is to say in the course of the morning, nobody had taken exception to my yellow trousers and I had got used to them. In fact, I was presumptuous enough to think that in a few years' time long trousers would have become the summer wear of the Dolomite world. The old man pushed himself into our circle. I judged him to be about sixty, perhaps older. He was wearing trousers of a conventional cut and pattern, a mountain hat and a rucksack which would have done justice to a younger climber. And there stood I in my ochre-coloured trousers, no hat, no rucksack and no rope, in fact lacking everything, in the centre of a bunch of about twenty first-rate climbers. Only the badly worn toes of my climbing boots indicated that I was one of them. I glanced down at myself and began to feel a little ridiculous. My mother had washed the trousers before I wore them and on the way down from Base Camp it had snowed and they got dirty. They were clean now, but the knees were lighter in colour where they had worn.

The Padua students said goodbye and promised to send me the newspaper which had printed my obituary notice. But the old man did not want to know.

'Ten minutes ago, you were up there on the ridge?'

'Has that anything to do with the newspaper?' asked one of the bystanders.

'No, because of the yellow trousers,' interjected the old man.

'I was on the North Ridge of the Second Tower,' I said shortly.

'Quite alone?'

'Alone.'

'And no rope?'

'No rope.'

'It made cold shudders run down my back,' he said irritably, toying with his binoculars as he spoke. He pointed out to the others the way up the airy ridge. 'I could hardly keep up with him, he was climbing so quickly. He's quite mad, I have never seen anything like it.' Sadly shaking his head, he went on his way. Yes, today up there I rose up from the dead, at least as far as the Padua climbers were concerned.

This morning I started climbing early and for my first climb chose the Jahn Route on the Third Sella Tower. The Jahn Route is one of my favourites. I was soon at the traverse and noticed that some parties were staring at me. As I got nearer I saw that they were friends. I waved and smiled. They were not expecting this encounter so I went on, up and down by the normal route. As I walked along the base of the Towers in the cirque, it happened. Some climbers were standing there and looked at me pensively. Two more abseiled down from the North Face. Suddenly one of them stood stock still and looked at me as though I were a ghost. When I greeted him, he didn't reply. It was Gianni Mazenga, the best climber of Padua. We used to be good friends and had done two winter climbs together. I just could not understand his attitude. The others also stood there and looked me up and down without saying a word. I looked just as I had always done, maybe the trousers were different and perhaps the beard, otherwise I

The Yerupaya Grande (6634m) in the Peruvian Andes. On the right is the North-East Face, after which Reinhold Messner began his sequence of successful ascents in the Alps.

had not changed at all. And yet these friends of mine from Padua stood there, visibly startled, as I approached. I went up to them with a broad grin and shook their hands.

I told them all about the Andes, but they seemed to follow my account of the climbs with difficulty. The one-sided conversation was slowly drying up, when one of them suddenly blurted out:

'We thought you were dead!'

I laughed and someone said that a rumour had got around in Padua; it was supposed to have been in the papers: Terrible tragedy, two dead and two bad cases of frostbite . . .

Meanwhile Gianni had recovered. It took him a long time before he could believe that I really was alive. We had been talking for half an hour, so I asked one of them to accompany me up the North Ridge. They looked at one another, looking quizzical; no, not with a dead man . . . anyhow it is too late and also too cold.

I started up alone and felt the rock under my hands. Each metre was different, sometimes the holds were large and my body could lean outwards, then again there were cracks large enough for my arms and feet. Soon the ground under me seemed to flatten out, thick woods below, the road looked like a black strip and the cars like toys. The top part of the face was the steepest. I leant well back and felt content and at peace with the world.

When I got back to the Sella Pass road, I noticed that they were all standing where I had left them. They invited me to come into the hut with them and celebrate my resurrection . . .

I did not devote this summer to undertaking big ascents and still less was I bent on breaking records. It was always my practice to climb some of the classical routes before I ventured on a severe climb and thus I often returned to some of my old favourites, which I knew from previous expeditions. It was precisely solo climbing of third, fourth and fifth grade climbs which supplied the rhythm which was lacking when I climbed with others or extended myself to my physical limit. I was able to pay more attention to technique and to the freedom of movement which is the essence of enjoyable climbing. If I found myself climbing clumsily, frightened or even just tired on severe rock, I rapidly regained my self-possession after a few easier climbs. I never attempted a very severe climb in the spring, at the beginning of the season.

Every summer, like this one, I began with a recapitulation of my climbing progress, in fact the progress of alpinism itself. It only takes at the most one or two months to run right through the whole range, from easy climbs up to those of the sixth grade. I was able to shorten this period somewhat by organised training, but I took care never to exceed it.

In the City of Stone

My brother, Günther, and I took it in turns to practise on a rock face eight metres high, situated in the 'City of Stone'. This was essential for our finger training. The holds were covered with grease and earth and the more we slipped off, the harder we tried. We had spent more than an hour on this crag and we had no intention of giving up. The valley lay in shadow and the air was as cool as the rock itself. The bright light of the midday sun shone down on the collection of rocks known as the City of Stone which lay to the left of the road leading up to the Sassolungo.

I wriggled my arms and yawned lazily. My brother also straightened up, yawned and smiled at me. During the morning we had been driven off the South Buttress of the Innerkofler Tower by a storm, so we roped off and came over here.

We gave up training and picked up our pullovers, and ambled up to the Comici Hut.

As the weather looked as if it would be fine for a bit, we started up the North Ridge of the Sassolungo, climbing unroped. Although Günther had been training every day and had great first ascents in mind, great climbs of middling difficulty were his favourites, such as the classical Dolomite climbs – the Fehrmann Route on the Campanille Basso, the Kiene Crack on the Punta della Cinque Dita, the North Face of the Saas Pordoi, the Schleier Ridge on the Punta Fiames and many others. We could name them by the hundred, each one different and none inferior to another. When we felt in particularly good form, we chose climbs like Micheluzzi's

The three Sella Towers in the Dolomites. The North-West First Direct on the Second Tower is one of the finest climbs in this region. The North Bridge is on the right.

routes on the Piz de Ciavázes and the Fiames Ridge . . . perhaps even the South-West Face of the Cima Scotoni, the Castiglione-Vinatzer Route on the Marmolata di Rocca or the Phillip-Flamm Route on the Punta Tissi.

Big ice climbs depend so much on the prevailing conditions. We were so enthralled by the Sulden Ridge on the Punta della Cinque Dita that I tried it again ten days later. This time I had more than enough of it – verglas in places, slush and generally dangerous. It had changed out of all recognition in the course of a few days.

The North Face of the Courtes has scarcely its equal in the Alps . . . or has it? There are still the Valais, the Bernese Oberland, the rocks of the Kaisergebirge, the Berchtesgaden Alps, all dream tours. In reality I knew so few of them. The Roggal Ridge, I was told, is particularly fine; I should have loved to try it.

So many climbs, so many desires. I was often asked, which was my favourite climb. It might have been any one of a dozen. There was nothing tangible on which I could lay my finger and say, 'That's the one' or 'It could be this one'. I just could not make up my mind and in any case I wanted to be free from being tied down to a once-for-all decision.

I had no conception of a favourite climb, I just allowed myself to be surprised by the mountain. This happened to me on the first ascent of the North-East Face Direct of the Second Sella Tower, on the new South Face Route on the Marmolata or on the North Face of the Cima della Madonna. One face might be superior to the others as regards elegance and beauty and yet I could not rate one higher than another. Three first ascents – and each one taken as a whole was a maximum achievement. This may sound like boasting, perhaps I was only remembering the best aspects of the climbs . . . who knows?

Günther was making the fourth ascent of the North Ridge of the Sassolungo. He knew the way down well, so that we were back in the City of Stone by late afternoon, in plenty of time to solve a few more face problems even though they were only a few metres high.

54

Before I left for the Andes, I added a picture postcard and a route description of the North Face of Les Droites to my file on the ENSA climbers' meet in Chamonix.

I had had my eye on this face for some time but did not quite know how to put my plan into effect. I read the description again which ran as follows:

'This face poses the greatest problem in the area of the Argentière Glacier. For a mixed rock and ice face, the average angle of 59·5° (for 1000m) of a face of 1080 metres is unusually high. According to the account of the first ascent, the party must have come up against exceptionally bad conditions. Even given good conditions one would have to reckon with one or two bivouacs on the face.

'The actual North Face of the Droites is bounded to the east by the buttress descending from the East Summit (4000m) and to the west by the buttress coming down from the West Summit (3984m). Both buttresses and the North Face between them are clearly marked on the Vallot Map.

'Leaving the Argentière Hut, proceed in a south-westerly direction over the Argentière Glacier to the foot of the face. Cross several crevasses at the foot of the great ice face lying to the right-hand side of the lowest slabs. This first portion of the face, which starts off at an angle of 60°, very soon eases off. Halfway up the face, a horizontal traverse to the right leads to the bottom half of a rock spur (first bivouac). Two rope lengths up this spur ice is encountered once more, where a dièdre is formed by the junction of the North Face and the rock spur. Twenty-five metres of very steep ice (70°). After a pitch of about ten metres of slightly less steep rock, the angle of the face increases again (second bivouac at the foot of a very steep vertical slab). It is advisable to follow a completely ice-filled crack to the right

55

of this slab, as the face increases in steepness and would appear to be absolutely vertical for a distance of seventy metres.

'*Three run-outs on completely verglased rock with a few meagre cracks (V and A1), then over an eight metre ice bollard to the third bivouac site.*

'*Ascend the very steep mixed rock and ice face towards the East Summit. Fourth and fifth bivouacs on this part of the face.*'

Only Half an Hour's Sleep

First Solo Ascent of the North Face of Les Droites

I was invited to take part in the International Climbers' Meeting of the ENSA in Chamonix from 17 July. I had no hesitation in accepting and set off at once. My father and mother came along as well. They wanted to take advantage of the fine weather and combine the journey with a visit. Three of my brothers were spending the summer at the Alp Albin in Switzerland. They were earning pocket-money for the school months, Erich as a cowherd, Siegfried as an assistant cowherd and Hubert as a shepherd.

The drive via Milan, Chivasso and Aosta went by in a flash. Father told anecdotes of the weeks he had spent there in the war when retreating in Italy. He still recognised some of the villages, although much had changed in the meantime. From Courmayeur we saw Mont Blanc for the first time, the sun was shining on the huge snowfields of the Brenva flank and I thought I detected a snow plume on the summit.

As we were following the queue through the tunnel to France I kept thinking of the Frêney Pillar. I was still immersed in my thoughts up there above the tunnel when it came to an end and before us lay Chamonix, the climbers' town.

We listened to the weather report in Chamonix; it was good but I had no climbing companion. We wandered through the town observing the summit slopes of Mont Blanc in the last rays of the setting sun. The glowing summit looked friendly above the already

57

Les Droites in the Mont Blanc Range. North-East Face to the left, North Face to the right. The latter was then considered to be the most difficult rock and ice face in the Alps.

dark and gloomy Aiguilles de Chamonix. I could not, however, restrain a feeling of awe as I regarded the tormented glaciers creeping slowly down the mountain into the valley.

It was that evening that I discovered my predilection for the North Face of Les Droites. I cannot remember having ever conceived the idea before of attempting a solo ascent of this formidable wall, but now, as the sun was going down, I made up my mind. At that moment I could envisage the dark face and the serrated ridge gleaming in the sunlight and felt drawn towards it. I was surprised nobody else had thought of attempting a solo ascent.

I felt I wanted to walk, jump and run. Nobody mentioned the face, they were all going about absorbed in their own thoughts of holidays, of the office or the factory. They smoked their cigarettes and downed drinks at the bar. I felt I had to get out of everybody's way in case they guessed my intentions from the look on my face.

Next day we drove to Argentière and I went up to the basin bearing its name. My parents drove on to see my brothers in Switzerland.

It had already gone ten o'clock as I crossed the flat glacier under the Aiguille Verte. The sun was burning down and the heat was reflected from the snow. A small stream bubbled alongside the dirty footmarks.

A man in front of me kept wiping his brow with his shirt sleeve, then he stood still, stooped down and drank greedily from the icy water. There was a subdued roar high up on the face. The man looked up as though somebody had called his name and then went on quenching his thirst.

Some stones, loosened by the sun on the summit ridge, clattered down the wall. I shrank back as though they had hit me. Splinters bounded down the smooth ice wall, leaving small, bright marks behind.

I must be on the vertical part of the face by eight o'clock, I thought, otherwise I shall have to turn back.

Silence returned to the Argentière Basin. I scanned the face again. The incredibly steep bulge at the start was smooth; from a recess in the middle of the wall a narrow strip of snow led upwards to the first rock islets. Above them the face steepened until it became vertical. Fresh snow lay on the tops of the buttresses and rays of sunlight were just appearing on the summit crest.

Half an hour later I forced my way into the crowded hut. Some guides stood about. I dropped my gear on the floor and went into the kitchen to see Michel. He grinned all over his face as I shook his hand. 'Les Droites?' he asked and then, 'Where's your brother?' I shook my head, 'I'm alone.'

Michel was the guardian's son and had been my friend for a long time. We got to know each other in August 1965 – he was only a kid then. He was, however, the only one in the hut who spoke German. Since then he had become a medical student, otherwise he had not changed at all.

Günther and I had had a go at the face four years before but gave up after 200 metres.

'You must come back for the North Face,' Michel had said as we parted. And now here I was. 'Les Droites,' said Michel again. I nodded. He looked pensive. 'Alone?'

'Yes, I'm going to try.'

'It's difficult.'

'I know that, I'm only going to try.'

Michel suddenly laughed and became quite enthusiastic about my proposition.

'Don't let on!' I said, 'and keep an eye on the face tomorrow.' Michel picked up his binoculars. Later on he showed me my bed and returned to the kitchen. I packed my sack, put it on the blankets and returned to the kitchen downstairs.

Apart from Michel's brother, I didn't know anybody. Surreptitiously I took the hut book, sat down at a table and leafed through the pages.

Close to me a guide was sitting and talking. Everybody there was listening to what he had to say. Although I did not understand any French, I gathered that he was talking about my proposed solo ascent. I stood up, put down the book and without looking round

The lower part of the North Face of Les Droites is a very severe
ice climb, the upper part is interspersed with rock. Nearly all the climbers
who attempted this face failed, before Reinhold Messner climbed it.

went outside. Michel was standing on the verandah, but I could not be cross with him. Silently he handed me his binoculars. I took them and looked up at the face. Michel's small brother turned up and grinned. Later on we went into the dormitory and checked over my equipment again.

Michel got a file and we all went out of the hut in order to sharpen my crampons. The guides who were sitting there exchanged a quick glance, which did not escape me. One of them patted me on the shoulder as they went in for their evening meal.

Only Michel was left, he came and sat by me on the verandah. Now that darkness was coming on, I began to feel a little dubious. 'Michel,' I said, 'I won't go tomorrow.' As he seemed surprised, I said I would have a try, but I had not made up my mind.

That night I could not sleep, I kept going to and fro from the dormitory to the living room, and back again. There were some people in the latter, so I slunk away and went back to bed. Gradually the hut quietened down, then someone shut a window. A night in a hut like any other, but still I could not sleep. Thinking about the face had spoilt my peace of mind. Michel had promised to wake me. 'I'll do the North Face of the Verte,' I said. 'Wake me with the others.'

I lay under the blankets and tried to will myself to sleep, but it was no good. Was it too hot or stuffy, or was it Les Droites Face which kept me awake? I looked at the time, which first of all seemed to drag, now it raced. My thoughts in my state of semi-wakefulness were right – were wrong – were neither right nor wrong, like everything else one thinks about when half asleep.

Michel woke me up with the early morning starters at one o'clock – this startled me although I had not slept.

Two o'clock – more went off. Where to? Argentière, Verte, Triolet, perhaps even Les Droites? Michel shone a light on me. I shook my head.

My eyes were open now; somewhere a candle made shadows on the wall. I had stopped thinking and just lay there, listening to the breathing alongside me.

Minutes of numbed confusion, minutes of indecision, minutes without aim or will-power. I lay there and my thoughts circled around in my head like will-o'-the-wisps. It was all most peculiar.

Michel pulled my blanket. I pretended that I had gone off to sleep, but now I was no longer in that empty blind alley where my thoughts had aimlessly wandered.

When all the parties had set out, I got up, dressed, picked up my sack and slipped out into the night.

There were three lights heading for the Triolet North Face. A guide lit his lamp; dawn was slowly breaking in the east. As I stumbled down the slope leading towards the glacier basin, I again toyed with the idea of Les Droites North Face. I was at the top of my form, the weather was good and I had not a care in the world. During the night everything seemed unreal, but now all doubts had vanished. Freed from uncertainty, I began my approach to the start of the face.

I sank up to my ankles in the snow. The lights on the Verte Face were high now, there must have been six or eight of them. Day broke as I stood below the bergschrund. The start was vertical and severe. I found a groove to the left which led me up to the snow slope above it. I then ascended obliquely upwards to the right to the foot of the first rock pitch. A thin film of verglas covered the slabs, which reared up above me in a frightening manner.

The Face had only been climbed three times before and the parties had taken anything from two to five days to accomplish it. Above the next piton the slope seemed to ease off, if only I could get there . . .

It gave me a kick not to have to bring my thoughts to a final conclusion, for I could always go down!

I was quite aware, however, that I had no time to waste. I must either reach the summit rocks or be clear of the face by eight o'clock, for about that time stones would start falling. I could not rely on chance, only on my condition and on the calculations made the day before based on my observation of the face. I knew only too well that stones would begin to fall as soon as the sun touched the summit rocks. The formidable cleft ahead of me was completely smooth. However, the ice was relatively soft and the crack was so deep that I was able to jam myself into it. I climbed continuously, relying on the front points of the crampons which I rammed hard into the ice. I had an ice axe in my right hand and a long spike in my left, which I drove into small clear spots in the ice.

Even when climbing on ice I adopted the well-known principle of three firm points of contact; when I had obtained good support with the axe and the spike, I advanced three steps. Owing to the angle of the face, I could not cut steps without losing both rhythm and balance.

At last, after about a hundred metres, the face eased off somewhat and I was able to take a breather. I then continued climbing, one rope paid out behind me and the other on my back. Just below the rocks at the beginning of the last section of the face I tied it on. I had barely taken two hours from the bergschrund to this point and so far not a single stone had fallen from above.

I climbed over mixed terrain obliquely upwards to the right and just below an overhang I belayed myself with my two long ropes. The rock hereabouts was inclined to be slabby and all the cracks were full of ice. Only once did I come across a piton, which must have been left in by Wolfgang Axt and Werner Gross on the second ascent of the Face.

Slightly higher up I deviated too far to the left and lost the Axt variant, however I took the line of least resistance. The original route ran further to the right, but appeared to me to be too dangerous owing to the prevailing verglas.

The way ahead was barred by a steep holdless slab. To the left it was quite impossible and the rock on the right was too rotten. I could have climbed back to the Axt variant but preferred to try the crack about as wide as a hand which bisected the granite slab. As I had only two sufficiently large channel pitons with me, I drove in the first one and, belaying myself to it, climbed up as far as I could. I then inserted the second one and roped down from it

Climbing on granite on the 'Pilier Bergland' on the North-East Face of Les Droites. The legs are spread wide apart in order to afford more free-play for the upper part of the body.

in order to recover the lower piton. Between the pitons I used knotted slings when necessary, which meant the sacrifice of a piece of my longest rope.

I spent a lot of time and attention on this slab. It was more than a rope's length and very difficult. I made five attempts on it before I was able to get to the top. A ramp now led obliquely upwards to the right, back to the route of the first ascent. Here, powder snow, lying on top of the ice, demanded extreme caution. I did not feel secure until I had anchored myself to the inadequate knobs of rock and could dig the points of my crampons into the ice. Suddenly, when I was standing on a slab of ice covered with snow, I realised how much my calves were aching. Overcome with sleep, I sat down on a small boulder protruding from the ice like a pulpit, tied myself onto a piton and promptly fell asleep.

When I awoke I was not quite conscious of my whereabouts. I was startled as I glanced down the ropes to the depths beneath. I was on the North Face of Les Droites, about 900 metres up. I did not want to wake up, I closed my eyes and tried to doze. I felt that sleep was the most wonderful thing in the world but I could not sleep any more. Down below on the glacier I could see two men. The sun must be exactly due south for they were in the shadow of Les Droites. I pulled off my right glove and hauled in the rope.

Once more I calculated distances and the steepness of the slope. Another hour to the summit, I thought, and stood up. I was fully rested now. I made an oblique upwards traverse of an icefield, which I left where a steep wall interspersed with rocks led upwards towards two gendarmes on the summit crest. From below, these two dark rocks had looked like horns. With both hands on the rocks and the crampons biting into the ice, I climbed through the gap between the horns and reached the summit.

It was one o'clock and the sky to the south was completely cloudless. I started off down a gully and tried as far as possible to steer a course between the crevasses. However, owing to these crevasses and the fact that I was alone, this was the most difficult part of the whole trip. The snow was sodden like a thick soup and whenever I suspected a crevasse below me, I crawled on my stomach.

As I reached the edge of the glacier I suddenly felt a lump in my throat. I wanted to pull myself together and tried to laugh. Just over there was the hut. I lay down in the grass by the side of a spring by the path. Again my throat seemed to close up; if anybody had come over to me from the hut, I would have avoided them. It was many years since I had cried. I used my rucksack as a pillow. Something had suddenly broken inside me, I had the feeling of being freed from I knew not what. I did not think any more but I realised that my tears had restored my normal clear balance of mind.

A great climb of this nature is like a life unto itself – another life, a life separated from this world with its problems and its worries; and afterwards, shortly afterwards, the old life returns, without my wishing it, as though nothing had ever happened. Nothing has really happened; only a piece of the jigsaw is missing.

The vital energy from the combustion in the body, and the resistance it encounters in the form of difficulties, maintain an equal balance until I am down again.

where else. It is like a story and sometimes I am not sure whether it is a part of my life or not.

The Frêney Pillar on Mont Blanc is one of these climbs; it is the most difficult ascent to the roof of Europe. Four first-rate climbers perished on the first attempt in the summer of 1961. For days they were subjected to a terrible storm which held them up below the Candle, the crux of the ascent. Then they came down, plagued by hallucinations, with badly frost-bitten hands and feet. Walter Bonatti led the descent, blazing a trail in the deep snow, helped by Pierre Mazeaud. Four out of the original seven died from exhaustion, delirium and the effects of lightning.

The first ascent was made soon afterwards and was repeated several times. But the Pillar will always be a serious undertaking and one must reckon on two days from the La Fourche bivouac to the summit.

The granite buttress on the Frêney Face of Mont Blanc.
The compact middle buttress, the Central Pillar, is considered one of the
most difficult routes up Mont Blanc.

Ascent of the Central Pillar of Frêney in a Single Day

When I got back to Chamonix, Erich Lackner was waiting for me. He had just returned from the West Face of the Petites Jorasses and was bursting with energy.

Erich is a large, sturdy man and came to mountain climbing by way of boxing. His arms and hands reveal immense power. He is naturally a good-natured man and probably gave up boxing for that reason. He was at this time studying mathematics and physics at Vienna University. He is exactly the type who, according to statistics, would fall off on his first serious climb. He had, however, accomplished hundreds of severe rock climbs without the slightest mishap, before he accepted the invitation to the ENSA (École Nationale du Ski et d'Alpinisme) meet in Chamonix.

The day after I came down from Les Droites North Face, we went up to the La Fourche fixed bivouac, with the intention of climbing the Central Pillar of Frêney.

That same evening we had a good look at the glacier basin which flows beneath the huge Brenva Flank towards the North-East Face of the Aiguille Blanche. Despite this, we had considerable difficulty next morning in not losing our way. Two parties bound for the Route Major started out with us. We descended gullies and snow slopes and crossed the flat basin below the south flank of Mont Blanc. It was so dark that we were unable to pick out the ribs and buttresses of the immense face above us. Frequently we mistook the lights of climbers above us for stars. During the ascent up the steep couloir to the Col de Peuterey, we became involved in a maze of crevasses, which we were unable to get round until dawn broke behind the Grandes Jorasses.

We chased each other up the wall, belaying from time to time and crossing a number of crevasses. The snow was hard on the Col and the sun shone directly on the three massive Frêney Buttresses, imparting a pleasing tone to the granite. The long bergschrund winding along the foot of the wall had shown only two weak spots. We aimed for the left-hand one, crossing the intervening plateau by means of a rather vague track. The July sun had softened it so that the footmarks, filled with snow granules by the night frost, were scarcely visible.

The sun was becoming stronger every minute and toned down the red aspect of the granite walls above us. The air, which had been cold and clear, was now pleasantly warm and shimmered over the rocks.

Suddenly we heard a voice floating down to us from the gigantic smooth rock buttress above. At first we could only distinguish isolated words, now we heard requests for rope. We strained our necks but could not make out any party on the mountain. At the top of the Pillar, where the rock bulged outwards, the air was so still and clear that we could plainly make out every crack on the Face. 'There, there's someone hanging from the big overhang,' called Erich excitedly. I saw him at the same time. He was dangling in the air about 600 metres above us; every now and then the rungs of his étrier glinted in the sunlight. The tiny figure shook and quivered as though suffering from convulsions, then suddenly swung back from the roof of the overhang and hung suspended in the air like a sack. He has fallen, I thought. He did not move for a long time, then he pulled himself together, re-ascended the rope, stretched his legs and in two movements reached the stance just above him. He had taken more than an hour to overcome this key point at over 4700 metres. The two men, who were Bulgarians and also guests of the ENSA, told us that evening in the Vallot Hut that they had started their climb on the same day as I had attacked the North Face of Les Droites.

Climbing the Candle on the Central Pillar of Frêney. Lackner and Messner were the first to climb this formidable buttress without a bivouac.

It was now 6 am and the first rocks, coated with a thin ice glaze, lay just above us. The sun had just reached the first dièdre and from time to time pieces of ice broke off and clattered down the wall, disappearing into the bergschrund. We had started up the wall at the side of the buttress, following the cracks and dièdres until some coherent slabs permitted us to traverse across to the right. We ascended the edge of the buttress, taking turns to lead, until a piton lured me away to the right onto an extremely steep pitch. Before long I found that I could neither advance nor retreat.

With considerable difficulty I was able to move upwards from my stance to a small pulpit. Climbing with infinite care, I managed to lodge the toes of my boots on some tiny ledges, emerged from behind a projection and stretched out my right hand towards a round, protruding knob of rock. Two metres above, the slope eased off a little. I hung on for a few moments while looking for better holds. Clinging to tiny cracks and breathing hard, I was just able to retreat before it was too late. I remained for some time on the small pulpit, conscious of the fatigue in my arms, and did not dare to make a second attempt. Luckily I was able to hammer a piton into a small crack below me, so that I could at least belay Erich. He did not ascend to my stance but remained on the edge of the buttress from where he was able to overcome this very severe pitch. By midday we had reached the bottom of the Candle, after negotiating a completely holdless slab. The Bulgarians, in the meantime, had overcome the main difficulties and were on their way to the summit. We could now only rarely hear their shouts.

Suddenly we caught sight of a Yugoslav party, away over to the left on the Hidden Pillar (Harlin-Frost Route). We were about the same height as they but still had the main difficulties ahead of us. Their second man talked to us, although he was standing in a waterfall. It was not long before they had completed the second ascent of their route.

Erich led the first run-out on the Candle. He vigorously lay-backed up a detached flake, taking care not to put too much weight on the pitons, and took up a stance just below a big overhang. It fell to me to carry out a right-hand traverse under the great roof. Standing in an étrier, I watched him ascend the crack up to the roof itself. With his legs straddled, he crept up the crack which bisected the roof, jamming himself tight with his arms, while his legs dangled in the air.

Everything was so still that I could hear every sound – his breathing, his curses . . . The granite in the base of the crack was split and rotten, it was lucky that the pitons held. Bits of rock clattered down hundreds of metres, clear of the face. They landed far below, split into tiny pieces and rolled further down the wall, until they ended up on the dirty white avalanche cone at the bottom. Below the pallid snowfields spread the sea-green woods.

The sky was still cloudless, it was getting clearer towards the south and heavy mist lay in the valleys.

Falling stones once more disturbed these minutes of silent meditation.

Erich wriggled upwards in the crack, leaning outwards until he found two good holds on the left-hand edge of the roof. He had got over the worst; the following passages caused us no more difficulty and we reached the summit of Mont Blanc just as the sun was setting. Its shadow lay like a monstrous cone over the earth. The north slopes were bathed in a soft light below us. We threw down our sacks. I was able to stow away quite a lot of pitons, which had withstood knocking in and pulling out, into the outside pocket. Only a few pieces of line were left.

The aims of mountaineering lie outside the scope of direct material interest or individual satisfaction in the necessities of life. It has its meaning within itself. Movement and innovation, the raising and lowering of tension and the combination of difficulties and their solution, all tend to make climbing like a game. This is particularly true of a first ascent: one is committed beforehand, it is limited by time and place and cannot be repeated.

Only when I felt myself to be in particularly good form did I attempt an unclimbed route, in order to solve it in a manner as stylish and as practical as possible. I do not much hold with first ascents which are carried out in stages, or new routes prepared in the summer, so that they can be carried out in the winter or the following summer. If I was not able to complete a climb, I abseiled off and took my ropes with me.

Also I will have nothing to do with climbs depending upon expansion bolts or a block and tackle. If I could not get by without employing such methods, I was prepared to give up and leave the solution to others.

Granite and Snow

First Ascent of the 'Pilier Bergland' on Les Droites

It is a formidable buttress. I had noticed it from the moment when Michel, later that afternoon, had remarked, quite casually, that it was unclimbed. I had intended to do something on the Aiguilles or on the Brenva Face, but we were in fine form and we were used to climbing on granite.

I knew the Argentière Basin very well and it was quite by chance that I had not become aware of this buttress before. It is slightly hidden but not remote. Erich pointed to a large rock tower in the middle of the face – an excellent site for a bivouac. We packed and repacked our sacks three times, so that next morning when we started off, we had only got the bare necessities with us. We did not, however, stint ourselves of bivouac equipment, taking food for some days, rock and ice gear, two ropes, maps and a compass.

The climbing was difficult from the start. Above the bergschrund I wrestled with a virtually holdless slab. Suspended from a 'knife-blade' piton, I swung over to the left and gained a little height by clinging to tiny irregularities on the surface. 'Watch out,' I called, 'there aren't any holds.'

With great care and relying on balance, I felt for any existing rugosities. The pitch was not steep and the smallest crack would have helped. The coarse-grained granite was overlaid with sparse lichen and was slippery so that I had to take great care in placing my feet. As I had no holds, I could not afford to slip. The quartz grains protruding from the rust-brown surface were not sufficient to hold my fingers so that I could take an upward step. The buttress, still at the same angle, reared above me. Far above it was bathed in sunlight.

At last I was able to call down, 'I've made it', as I finally overcame this holdless slab. It had been a question of friction and balance.

We changed over the lead now and climbed up an icy crack, traversing to the right and up the sharp edge of the buttress. Here the face was unusually steep but broken up so that there were plenty of large hand- and foot-holds.

Utilising a system of grooves, we reached the top of the tower which we had previously selected for our bivouac site. We did not stop, however, but traversed to the left into a series of cracks, through which we attained the crest of the buttress. From below the terrain often seemed unclimbable, but somehow we always managed to thread our way through. After climbing some more rock pinnacles, we eventually reached the summit.

We were in the middle of sorting out our gear when a small aircraft approached and circled twice round us. On board were guides from the ENSA meet who had come along to see how we were getting on. They waved to us as the machine disappeared behind the Aiguille Verte.

We descended the South Face of the mountain unroped. Just above the bergschrund, we had to traverse to the right as there did not seem any possibility of abseiling down. I had the ropes on my back and was standing a few metres above the edge of the crevasse and Erich was about forty metres above me on the lower edge of the rocks. The snow was soft owing to the bright heat of the sun.

I was just looking over the top lip of the crevasse which was about ten metres deep, when I suddenly heard a rushing sound. Erich had started off a snow slide which was coming straight for me and widening rapidly. I just had time to ram my axe into the snow with all my strength, praying that I would not be carried down by it. Then, quite unconsciously, I let out a cry of terror as I was carried over the edge and fell into the depths. I just remember wet snow falling on my head and knew no more.

About ten minutes later, I managed to free myself from the masses of snow. I was uninjured but had lost my axe. Then, some distance away, I heard Erich's voice:

'Are you hurt? Are you all right?'

'I've lost my axe,' I said, when I had climbed out of the bergschrund onto the glacier.

The object of coming to Chamonix was to climb mountains and, after we had done Les Droites, we had a day off. Our next objective had been the rather indeterminate Hélène Buttress on the Grandes Jorasses. However, we arrived at the start of the climb too late and were surprised at the bergschrund by a terrific fall of stones. The preceding night had been too warm, so we therefore gave up this planned first ascent and went back to Chamonix.

When we got there we learned of the death of Jörg Lehne. He was killed by stonefall at the foot of the Walker Spur. His companion, Karl Golikow, was in hospital with severe injuries, so Erich and I went to visit him.

Karl spoke to us about Jörg and as I listened, I conjured up memories of him. 'I knew him,' I said during a pause in the conversation. I had secretly admired him, but I did not say so now.

'That's how it happened,' said Karl, moving slightly and groaning with pain.

'Yes,' he said again, 'it was just like that', as though he couldn't understand what had happened. A misfortune is generally more incomprehensible for the person concerned than it is for a third party.

As we left, I could not help thinking that this might have happened to us on the Yerupaya Wall. Or on Les Droites. It could happen to me on any one of the great faces. I remembered how many of the great climbers had been killed over the past years: Louis Lachenal, Hermann Buhl, Jean Couzy, Toni Egger, Andrea Oggioni, Toni Kinshofer, Lionel Terray, John Harlin . . .

Suddenly I found myself involved in a macabre train of thought. How many of the first climbers of the Brandler-Hasse Route on the North Face of the Cima Grande were still alive? About half. Or of the conquerers of Nanga Parbat? One out of four. Or of the first party up the Eiger North Face . . . or of the ten best climbers of the last twenty years, three or four . . . I do not know what my friends thought about all this, but why should they think differently? Suddenly my presence in Chamonix seemed a trifle meaningless. It is true that I had always taken into consideration the possibility of being hit by a falling stone, but now the thought seemed somewhat depressing.

I had known Lehne but only superficially. I had dreamed of climbing with him and now he had thrown my dreams back at me.

Only Two Words in Common

First Ascent of the North Face of the
Pointes du Domino

Michel is French, he does not speak German, nor I French.

Every thirty minutes we took it in turns to break a trail. Neither of us spoke a word. It was hot and the snow was soft. Avalanches crashed down from the walls to the right and left of us, breaking the silent peace of the night. Everywhere crevasses lay in wait for us. It seemed as if even the narrow moraine ridges on the glacier were planning an ambush. A glacier stream emerged silently from the ice and flowed away into the darkness.

Only the faint gleam of the steep ice walls of the Triolet, the Courtes and the Domino penetrated the obscurity, dominating the glacier with their apparently invincible might. I was behind Michel and, with my rucksack in my hand, was trying hastily to take off my pullover. He suddenly stood still, turned round and exclaimed in his jovial voice:

'Grosse Scheisse!'

I had hardly taken in this unexpected sally, before he set off up an avalanche cone to the foot of the North Face of the Domino.

On the previous afternoon, Michel Marcel had persuaded me to make a first attempt on the North Face of the Domino. As it was too late to start going up to the hut, he asked one of his friends to fly us up to the Argentière Hut by helicopter.

I was enormously impressed by this flight. As we hovered past the North Face of Les Droites, it was so steep that it made my flesh creep. It is said that the Argentière Basin is surrounded by the finest and possibly the most difficult ice walls in the Alps. There they stand in all their glory: Verte, Droites, Courtes and Triolet, seemingly fighting for supremacy in height and steepness.

On the other hand, the North Face of the Domino stands to the left of the Triolet, comparatively humble and insignificant. It does not attract much attention beside its imposing neighbours and probably for this reason it had remained unclimbed.

From the helicopter, Michel pointed out the proposed route as far as was possible in our mixture of languages. He told me that parties had already attempted it, French for the most part. Shortly afterwards we landed just below the hut.

We remained awake until far into the night and set off at one o'clock, tired and sleepy.

'It's too warm,' I said. Michel did not understand, shoved his gloves into his pocket and let his axe swing from his wrist. He did not appear to be at all tired and was full of energy and confidence.

'Grosse Scheisse!' he said at the bergschrund.

'It's too warm,' I repeated, turning towards him. But he did not move from the spot and just went on quietly looking at the upper lip of the bertschrund, from which fell drops of water and icicles.

'It's impossible,' I said. From far above a stone came bounding down the slope. With commendable presence of mind we took cover under the lower lip of the crevasses. When it had passed we got on our feet again.

'Grosse Scheisse!' Apart from this terse remark, not another word passed his lips, but there was a restless and mettlesome glint in his eyes.

'It won't work,' I repeated, with a note of hopelessness in my voice, but Michel just smiled at me. Determined to call it a day, I threw down my sack in the snow and came down from the 'schrund. Michel followed and now even he appeared to be undecided. I knew quite well that if only I could explain things to him, he would also have doubts as to the wisdom of continuing. I therefore repressed my ill humour and tried to put an encouraging tone into my voice.

'Perhaps we can make it further along to the right.'

As he still remained silent, I gave him to understand that there was only one possibility – the overhanging ice chimney. We tramped back to our sacks and I pointed upwards.

Michel at once got to work and busied himself with his sack from which he extracted crampons, some pitons and a bag of dried fruit. He tied on the rope, put on his sack, toyed with his axe and waited.

I gave him a sign to go ahead but he just kept looking at the chimney.

'Grosse Scheisse!' I looked him deep in the eyes, but he turned away from me and stared fixedly at the wet, overhanging ice above. He was silent for a while and then turned to me and gave me an encouraging smile. He tried to laugh but was only able to produce a dismal grimace which looked most peculiar in the half light of the dawn.

'I'll have a go!' I said, realising that he had given up all hope.

'Direct?'

'Yes, it's the only possible way.'

'Grosse Scheisse!'

I climbed carefully up the chimney, trying to ward off my rising anxiety by talking to myself. Michel stood below, belaying me and not understanding a word. The ice was so soft that pitons would not hold. 'Bravo,' called Michel as I reached the rim of the crevasse.

Higher up I hacked out a small platform in the ice, inserted two screws and a long ice piton for good measure. Michel came up to me, handed over the ironmongery from his sack and indicated that he would like me to continue. I would have preferred him to lead the next run-out and offered it to him.

He bent back his head in order to estimate the angle of the face, which was about 60°, and smooth at that. When I saw his serious expression, I changed places with him and climbed obliquely upwards to the right. The front points of the crampons held well. We came together at the end of each rope's length and the higher we went the more our spirits rose. Further up, the condition of the ice was better and it was not so steep. We should reach the top by midday.

Michel led the first run-out on the rocks. His movements were calculated and precise, it was a pleasure to watch him.

As we stood on the summit a little later, we suddenly realised that we had left our passports in Chamonix.

'Grosse Scheisse!'

However, we went down the Italian side and reached Cour-mayeur hours later and were immensely relieved when the border guard let us through.

'Grosse Scheisse!' said Michel gratefully.

On the way home from Chamonix, we stopped off at Grindelwald. The weather was bad and the North Face of the Eiger was so covered in snow that we postponed our climb.

I started training two hours a day and found that in my track running I was a few minutes faster than after the Andes Expedition. At the first attempt I was able to accomplish the very severe eighty metre traverse at the old saw-mill three times without taking a rest. After a few days I increased this to four times. I had never been able to do this before. I reckoned that I was now fit enough to have a go at a solo ascent of the Philipp-Flamm Route on the North-West Face of the Punta Tissi.

I considered the Philipp-Flamm on the Civetta a counterpart in the Eastern Alps to the North Face of Les Droites, probably the most difficult mixed climb in the Western Alps. It is one of the most prodigious free climbs in the Alps, threading its way up 1000 metres of precipice with no possibility of deviation. I had climbed it before with Heini Holzer, so was quite aware where the principal difficulties lay and what equipment was necessary.

I took along karabiners in order to give myself an extra belay on the two artificial pitches.

I think little of artificial solo ascents. For this reason I have always chosen for my solo climbs routes which can be accomplished almost exclusively by free climbing. I am either too cautious or too lacking in courage to dispense with belays and trust to a mass of pitons. A satisfactory belay in solo artificial climbing is so complicated and time-wasting to achieve that the climb would forfeit its last vestige of finesse.

In the case of free climbing on the other hand, everything is quicker, more rhythmical and even easier. Naturally one must be in good condition and possess the know-how necessary to guarantee safe climb-

ing appropriate to the difficulties encountered. Basically I am a timid climber and have neither the courage nor the temerity to rely solely on luck.

In climbing circles I was considered as definitely mad when I ascended the Philipp-Flamm Route on the North-West Face of the Civetta, for previous ascents could be counted on the fingers of one hand. My critics gave me a month at the most and the only thing about which they were uncertain was where I would fall off.

The overhanging roof on the Philipp-Flamm Route on the Civetta. Many a first-class climber has lost his nerve at this crucial point of the climb.

The Obsession of an Unknown Objective

First Solo Ascent of the Philipp-Flamm Route on the Punta Tissi

Livio, the guardian, was standing outside the hut as I fastened the rope on my back.

'Werner,' I said to my little brother, who had come up with me last night to the Tissi Hut, 'Werner, I will be on top by four o'clock, so you can come to the Coldai Hut at five.'

I asked Livio to look at the face with his binoculars from time to time. He wanted to know where I was going.

'The Philipp-Flamm.'

'Alone?'

'Yes, alone.'

He sat down abruptly on the bench and did not say another word. The morning was well advanced – I had no time to spare.

'Ciao,' I said and ran down the slope, past several tents towards the start of the climb. When I turned round to wave, he was still sitting there. His eyes had a fixed expression, he had not taken it all in.

I jumped from rock to rock on the scree below the wall, stood still from time to time and looked up at the huge face. Mist clung to the rocks at the level of the snow triangle and the cracks were full of moisture. Now and again I could hear the voices of the Czech party which had started up about six o'clock.

It was now ten. I had come to the Civetta Group on the previous evening in the hope of meeting Vittorio Varale, a journalist and author, with whom I was working on a book. He was not there however and, apart from the guardian sitting in front of the hut, there were only two Dutch women present.

Despite all the horror stories which were told of the Philipp-Flamm Route, I had come here to attempt a solo ascent. The meeting with Varale was a pretext in order to put others off the scent. Although a solo ascent of the Philipp-Flamm had become an obsession with me, I wanted to keep it a secret – in fact I wished to convince myself that this was no unpremeditated adventure.

The first rope of the Czech party was in the act of traversing to the left into the base of the dièdre. Seen from below, the wall looked less vertical than it did from the Tissi Hut. But the great dièdre, set in the centre of the face, looked just as smooth and repellent. The crack at its back was dry but brittle in places. I felt a trifle uneasy.

Somewhere to the right I could hear the sound of waterfalls and stones kept falling on to the snowfield at the foot of the Solleder Route. The variant, which we had initiated two years ago, lay between the Solleder and Philipp-Flamm Routes. It was dry at the beginning of August; even on the summit rocks the ice appeared to have melted away. I was, therefore, not expecting waterfalls.

I climbed up the first cracks, which were scoured smooth by the action of water and falling stones. I made rapid progress owing to the low angle of the slope. I soon overtook the second Czech rope. The first couple had reached the point where the route takes a sudden turn to the left. I could not go on without inconveniencing them, so I remained at the stance until the second party had reached the same spot.

While waiting, I uncoiled one of my ropes, which trailed behind me like a long snake.

The Czechs kindly let me pass them at the next stance. Later on, when my rope got hooked up on a rock spike, I asked them to free it. They seemed reluctant to do so, some unpleasant remarks floated upwards and they suggested that I should come down.

The overtaking operation and the confusion of the ropes had upset me. I was no longer acting instinctively, I became impatient and tried to hurry. The movements of the other party had thrown me off balance. By that I do not mean body balance but mental co-ordination; instead of climbing the correct crack, I took the one next to it; when negotiating an overhang I lifted my foot too high and had to take it back. I lost the way, tried to the right, then to the left. It was not until I reached the beginning of the great dièdre, when the others were out of sight, that I reverted to normal.

It began to rain a little, but I went on. I reached the start of the yellow crack without a belay. I paused a moment on a ledge and looked down. The others had given up and had begun the descent. Large drops of rain were falling, but this did not affect me as I was below a big overhang. It will soon stop, I thought, as I worked my way up the smooth slab until I was able to enter the narrow crack. The dolomite rock on the left side of the crack was so smooth and polished that it shone. The rock became damp with the moist air and I could only retain my footing by placing my boots on small holds or nodules on the wall. I backed up against the overhanging wall, splinters of rock split off under me, but the holds held well under pressure.

Higher up, at one of the critical points of the climb, there was an expansion bolt. It was the second one I had found on the climb. Walter Philipp and Dieter Flamm of Vienna made the first ascent in 1957 without the use of bolts and very few pitons, and up to the end of 1966 no bolts were employed. It was not until the route became well-known and was attempted by parties not capable of coping with the difficulties involved that it became denigrated by the use of too many pitons and, above all, by this second expansion bolt.

A sporting or non-competitive spirit is a precondition for methodical and disciplined climbing. It is not easy to turn back in the middle of a face and for those persons lacking a sportsmanlike conscience, the saying 'It is much more difficult to retreat than to continue' is particularly relevant. This point of view means nothing to me. How many times have I renounced a great climb, because the weather turned bad, because I had not had enough training, or even because I had lost interest? Sometimes I was afraid to go on with it, another time I was too tired and on one occasion I was frightened of stonefall. I have always found it easy to retreat. Such was the case on a winter attempt on the Bonatti Route on the North Face of the Matterhorn, a solo attempt on the South-East Face of the Cima Scotoni and a retreat from near the summit of Demavend.

Retreat was in my mind when I reached the next crux, below the great roof. It cost me a great effort to get there. If necessary I could have roped down from where I was to the bottom of the wall in two hours, as a party before me had done when the leader was hit by a falling stone above the roof and came off. Blood still stained the rocks and a piece of rope hung from two pitons. I belayed myself by tieing two pitons together through which I ran the doubled rope. I attached the rope to my harness by a prusik knot and in this way hoped to keep a possible fall to a minimum.

Naturally I did not contemplate coming off. The many accident-free climbs which I had accomplished had given me confidence for a severe solo ascent of this nature. Nevertheless, the tension was great. Below the roof I traversed to the left on tiny holds, took off my belay when I reached the left-hand edge of the roof and climbed higher up the crack, until more overhangs forced me on to the slabs on the left. I traversed into the summit couloir somewhat higher than is stated in the route description. Although the rocks at this point were soaked with rain, I found them easy. Here I inserted two pitons, tied on my second rope and climbed the few remaining metres up to the couloir, as though I was in a roped party. Each time, before I took a fresh step, I pushed up the prusik knot on the belaying rope so as to shorten the free ends. From the upper piton, I roped back down to the stance, picked up my line from the last traverse and climbed back up the fixed rope taking my karabiner with me. I overcame all the artificial pitches in this manner.

As I drew in the rope, I was overcome by a horrible feeling of having irretrievably burned my boats. Any retreat from above the traverse was highly problematical, if not impossible. Now I had to go all-out for the summit. Two thirds of the face, on which I had spent something less than three hours, lay behind me. Ahead lay deep wet gullies, repellent and hostile.

I had underestimated the rain. A torrent was rushing down the gully above me and my long corduroy trousers were so wet that they restricted my movements.

Despite the damp air, I had a raging thirst. Rapid breathing and the exertion had dried up my body and I eagerly lapped up the brown water from the bottom of the smooth crack, taking care that it did not run down inside my shirt. I rapidly ate some fruit, for I knew what lay before me and realised that it would be a long time before I had another meal. Thick mist clung to all the surrounding mountains and now and then I thought I detected a few snowflakes mixed with the rain. I glanced down; it was much too late to think of retreating. Shivering slightly, I went on my way.

After a few easy steps I left the couloir on the right and found myself below the great overhang. This is regarded as the most difficult pitch on the climb and, recalling that some very good climbers had come to grief here in the past, I went hot all over as though fear had sharpened my perception.

The next pitch was steep and as the rock was very brittle, the piton at the start came away in my hand. I knocked it in more firmly and tied it to another one which I inserted myself and used them as a belay. The climbing at this point was extremely severe, added to which I could only utilise the holds for pressure.

I traversed to the right above the cave and reached a smooth and narrow crack. The rope had run out and as I tried to pull it up, it jammed. I pulled desperately at it with one hand while I held on to a flake with the other – it would not move. I swung the rope from side to side as far as my exposed stance would allow, pulled again, pulled until my left hand got cramp. This was dangerous, for strong fingers were essential for the next section of the climb, the summit couloir, more essential even than the perlon rope. Eventually I had to snap it through with the hammer and I was free . . . It was hailing now, heavily and steadily, and my clothes were dripping. I was in the summit couloir in the middle of a waterfall. I gazed anxiously into the dark canyon above me – it was grey, slippery and full of hail. Suddenly I heard an explosion overhead: lightning had struck. I hugged the wall and stones whistled past me. My movements were intuitive, completely automatic. Only instinct acquired over many years of activity can save one in such dramatic situations. Step by step, I clambered up the waterfall. To be really up against it creates its own terrors. There are many such ravines in the Dolomites, but for me there is only one like a strangler's hand.

I did not want to admit to myself that I was frightened. 'Straddle, spread your legs out,' I said to myself. Then with unwonted calm I began to knock in a piton. The water splashed down between my legs.

I was hoping to find shelter in a cave and frequently thought of a bivouac. But the cold was so intense that, after a short rest, I had to go on. I would never have withstood a night out under these wet and cold conditions, even in a bivouac sack. I had taken the precaution of stuffing my bivouac sack under my pullover before I left the hut, but I did not get it out because subconsciously I was still hoping that it would stop raining before nightfall.

I belayed myself very securely in that part of the gully which coincides with the Comici Route, examining each piton in order to see that there were no cracks in the eyes. My movements were impeded by my wet trousers and my clothes were sticking to my body. If I was forced to stand for long in the water while inserting pitons, I began to freeze up at once. I am a conservative climber and can make do with the simplest expedients. Neither expansion bolts nor down clothing would have helped me in my present predicament. Fortunately I was not over-indulged in this way and had learned to keep a clear head in the most difficult situations. In our technical age, being a little behind the times implies progress and safety.

I paused for a long time on the upper horizontal shelf below the chockstones. Fortunately I knew the route, so that I was able to find the way in spite of the thick mist. I managed to discover the exit hole at the top of this huge chasm, crawled through it and went on.

The mist was uniformly thick now and did not hold out hope for any improvement. Just once, in the terminal dièdre, when the rain had ceased for a short time, I was able to see the Tissi Hut far below.

My wet trousers were by now so heavy that I was afraid of losing them, so I took them off and tied them round my body. This considerably improved my movements over the last rope lengths. The ice-cold water which now ran over my bare legs did not trouble me as I was thoroughly hardened by the cold showers which I took daily at home. While I was climbing, I kept thinking of 'extravagant expressions' such as overhang, straddling, prusik knots and the like. Sometimes an idea occurred to me and a suitable form of expression would not come so that I could not carry it out. My instinct and my body were operating automatically but my mind was working slowly and I frequently mumbled to myself. I was quite aware of my dangerous situation and did not need to weigh it up, as I did the right thing instinctively. My eyes saw something, my hands reached out and my body made the correct movements without my having to think about it. If I had had to stop and think at every hand-hold, I would have been swept away by the water.

The short artificial pitch just below the summit, however, held me up long enough to make me shiver with the cold. But, as I hauled myself up the last few metres to the level gap between the Punta Tissi and the main summit of the Civetta, I began to warm up again. As I put on my soaking trousers, I was overjoyed to think that I did not need to bivouac.

At the bottom of the Via Ferrata degli Alleghesi, which I descended, I found a strange man waiting for me with a thermos full of tea and when I reached the Coldai Hut the guardian asked me to wait for the journalists who were coming up to the hut that evening to interview me.

I was not interested and went down with Werner. What answers could I give to their questions? Perhaps how I kept looking for cracks for the pitons under the waterfall and how I endeavoured to free the jammed rope? Or how the strange man had handed me the flask which he had obviously prepared specially for me and which he had carried for three hours up to the bottom of the face? Just that. As far as the public was concerned that was probably the only thing of note that occured on 2 August 1969.

At this period, my training consisted in the main of two parts. Firstly I kept up my general condition training and secondly I did a special kind of training to strengthen my fingers. Over the years we had worked out a traverse exercise at the old saw-mill which we kept up until our fingers got cramp, then we let go and fell off. This did not matter very much as the holds were, on average, not more than three metres above the ground. The traverse was about eighty metres long and I carried on until fatigue caused me to fall off.

On one occasion, just before the solo ascent of the Marmolata di Rocca, I managed to do six traverses without coming off. This was equivalent to 480 metres of climbing and, when one bears in mind that the holds were minimal, one can imagine the effort involved. Admittedly I knew every hold and movement intimately, but the most difficult metres after forty minutes of maximum effort were often a torment.

One thing I learned from this traverse at the old saw-mill was to be able to continue despite cramp in my forearms. For example, when I had taken the wrong route on the first solo ascent of the North Face Direct of the Cima della Madonna and got cramp when descending, my training was such that I could will myself not to let go. This, of course, required strong willpower but, above all, the knowledge that it would work.

This training did not take up too much of my time and I am convinced that, carried out over the years, it led to greater achievements.

Extreme climbing is perhaps one of the few sports which have, as yet, not reached the limit and which leave open the way to the attainment of completely new standards.

A Mysterious Face

First Solo Ascent of the North Ridge of the Sassolungo

I sat alone on the summit – the unmistakable summit of the Sasso-lungo. It could not have been long since the last climbers had had a meal there. Paper lay everywhere, stacks of it, remains of bread, a bottle full of dirty water, cheese rinds, orange peel dried up by the sun lay between the rocks and a little lower down lay a beer can which stank of urine.

I do not know why I did not tidy it up, but I was tired and ambled along the summit crest. As it was misty and evening was approaching, I pulled on my anorak so as not to catch cold. I had been climbing for several hours without a rest, except when I paused for a moment to knock in a piton. Whenever the sun managed to penetrate the mist, it was very glaring for the eyes although it was only weak. I turned my face towards it in order to get warm, screwed up my eyes and stood still.

As I turned round to go on I saw a face. At first I could not take it in. In the wall of mist close to me I distinctly saw a large head moving, surrounded by two large bright rings.

I stopped dead in my tracks, thought I must be mistaken and went on. But to my astonishment and horror, the face went on as well. When I stopped, it stopped too, rigid and apathetic, rather like a marionette which had slipped from the hand of the operator. When I turned, went on or stopped, it roused itself from its apparent lethargy and followed my every movement.

I ran now as one possessed along the jagged crest, followed by this unholy face. Never before in my life had I been able to find the start of the descent so quickly!

The Sassolungo from the north. The Yellow Nose to the left. The North-East Face Direct runs up the fall line of the black water channel in the centre.

The arête by which I reached the summit in barely three hours was more than 1000 metres in height. I started up at two o'clock to the left of the fall line of the Yellow Nose, having wasted the morning in trying to find the right start of the Soldà Route. To begin with I kept losing my way on the huge system of slabs and not until after 300 metres was I able to traverse out to the right immediately above the Nose, belayed by a piton, to the crest of the buttress. From this point I went straight up to the Pichlwarte and by late afternoon had reached the broken rocks of the summit by way of the chimneys and cracks of the original route.

I was so absorbed that I had not even noticed my surroundings and certainly had had no time to be frightened.

On the summit I began to wonder whether this was a new climb or whether I had followed an old route. In any event it was entirely suitable for free climbing and, although there was not a piton to be seen, it could well have been climbed by Paul Preuss.

Fleet of foot I ran along the summit ridge to the start of the ordinary route, sensing spectres behind me, followed and driven on by that face, by the filtering of the sunlight through the mist, by the smell of the rain-soaked rocks, by the wind . . . a deep ravine made me pause. Cautiously I glanced towards the wall of mist. And then, suddenly in the last red rays of the sun, I identified my own profile in this mysterious face.

Sometimes I wondered whether this summer could not have been different right from the beginning. And again I sometimes asked myself if I could not assume a different attitude towards life, at least as far as the future was concerned. It was nowhere stipulated that the life which I led was my own or that it must be exactly lived as I conducted it.

Mountaineering was not the 'usual' or 'real' life for me, it was rather an escape from it, a temporary activity which completely engrossed me. I regarded it neither as a moral duty nor as a physical necessity, but I would have found it difficult to give up. A mad crazy climb, on the other hand, could make me feel unpretentious, enthusiastic and ecstatic.

Mountaineering stands apart from moral functions, apart from wisdom and folly, from good and evil.

In the rhythm and harmony of a climb, the human body experiences an enhanced opportunity for expression, a proof of its existence.

Mountaineering is not bound up with any philosophy of life or civilisation, nor with financial prosperity, it is merely a question of having started to do it.

I was now studying again for a few hours every day, I visited exhibitions and bought books with the money I could have used to go to Mont Blanc.

Before I took a few days off for climbing, I now often asked myself if it would not have been better if I had done some more reading for my next exam. My more mature friends confirmed my doubts by saying, 'If you work hard now, you will have more time later on.' In order to back up their assertions, they used to point to their incomes and to their big business activities.

I understood their point of view but as soon as I had set off, I forgot all their petty pomposity.

Failure on the French Route (North-East Pillar on the Crozzon di Brenta)

I stopped the car just as the first raindrops fell on the windscreen. I had reached the pass just before Madonna di Campiglio and within a few minutes would arrive at the start of my proposed climb in the Brenta.

My rucksack lay ready packed in the car and, as I got it out, I noticed that mist was creeping up the valley from the west. The track wound its way up the mountain but on the whole I took short cuts between the bends. I levelled off after about an hour and then went downhill. It was already midday and the buttress was 1000 metres in height. I did not intend to bivouac.

As I ascended the last rise to the Brentei Hut, it began to drizzle, imparting a dingy colour to the rocks in the cirque. My shirt was damp from sweat and rain, I was alone without a hat and my anorak was in my sack. It was five hours since I had left home; I was driven on by a feeling of strength in my legs and my long-cherished desire to ascend the French Route no longer seemed irresponsible.

I toiled upwards with my eyes on the wall in front, cutting corners with a few powerful steps.

As dark heavy thunder clouds swept up the North Ridge of the Crozzon di Brenta, I stepped out and hastened up the last part to the hut. Pleased that I had got there before the rain, I threw my sack on the floor, got out my binoculars and studied the route.

I had run up the last part too quickly and was still too much out of breath to be able to make a detailed study of the face. I was dismayed to see fresh snow on the mountain. With the same speed with which I had decided upon this solo ascent, I now abandoned any idea of it. I thought it would be better to go down rather than wait here for an improvement in the weather.

Man's vitality is not solely dependent upon conscious will-power but is also effective in the form of vital instinct. This instinct for self-preservation is so great at moments of stress that it turns the mildest man into a wild animal and imparts a foreboding of danger. It is particularly foolish on a mountain to attempt to combat this instinct. What others call luck is frequently nothing less than the avoidance of preconceived misfortune.

This vital instinct is a part of the experienced mountaineer just as his expertise is. In point of fact, there is no absolute guarantee of safety on a mountain, no immunity against objective hazards. One must guide one's body up the climb and at all times do something to ensure maximum safety as far as possible.

On the descent it cleared up and the mist dispersed; soon the sun came out. At the bottom I took the right-hand path, walked up to the Tuckett Hut and then climbed the Kiene Route on the Casteletto Inferiore. I encountered a party close to the summit cairn. I had seen them earlier on by their car and had been rather taken by them. I said hullo and was about to pass by when they recognised me and asked me to descend with them, as otherwise they might be obliged to bivouac.

Over a glass of wine in the hut, they confessed that they had imagined me to be quite different: a large man with a brown face who did not drink. They were by no means the first who had said this to me.

'On the whole,' said one of them, as the guardian brought another glass of glühwein, 'on the whole, today was a great occasion.'

The wind lashed the rain against the window. If the weather had been good this morning, probably all three of us would have beeen in a bivouac tonight, I reflected.

At the time I was economically independent. My student's grant just sufficed for the nine months of lectures and for books. However, I ran a small car and did a lot of travelling, I had to work during the summer. I acted as a guide, gave lectures every once in a while and only went off on a big expedition when I had amassed a few lire for the purpose.

I enjoyed guiding as long as my clients were equal to the difficulties. I especially liked climbing with young people who, with their natural skill and sincerity, were fast learners.

If I had a client on the rope who was not up to the climb, his lack of skill rubbed off on me to a certain extent. As I watched him from my stance using loose rocks as holds and climbing with knees and elbows, I lost that rhythm and sense of safety which makes every movement automatic.

However, in such cases, a solo climb soon put me to rights.

As a Guide on the Cinque Torri

Ursula climbed the overhang on the South-West Face of the Cinque Torri better than I expected. I duly praised her and on the summit I wanted to know how she actually became a climber, for she had spent her childhood in East Prussia.

She told me that her parents had brought back pictures of Lake Lucerne and the Eiger from their holidays in Switzerland. She was very fascinated by these pictures and had hung them over her bed. Her parents told her about Chamonix and from then on mountains became an obsession with her. Filled with enthusiasm she began to ramble among the 'mountains' (not exceeding 300 metres in height!) of her homeland.

As a reward for a good school report, her mother took her on a trip to Bavaria, where she took the opportunity to climb the Zugspitze and Watzmann. She was so enthralled that she had only one thought in mind – to make prolonged excursions to the hills. But what excuse could she make?

She started taking lots of photographs, as though she intended to become a mountain photographer. This idea astonished her parents and was not approved by them. She eventually settled for becoming a dietician's assistant in Munich, which finally satisfied them.

She then entered upon a life full of experience. She got to know climbers and learned to climb. Her first objectives were climbing school, the foothills, the Karwendel and the Kaisergebirge. Means were limited, the approach marches long and the rucksack heavy. Before long she knew the Eastern Alps very well and the expeditions became longer and more difficult.

After she had finished her training, she intended to return to East Prussia. Before she did this, however, she made a trip to the Dolomites. This event stuck in her mind. The more distant she was from the mountains the more she missed them and the long journey – 1400 kilometres by car from Munich – did not prevent her from taking even longer trips.

Ursula married an East Prussian officer who accompanied her on her Alpine excursions. Then came the war, she became a widow, was evacuated and lost everything that she loved. She knew nobody and had to find a job – a holiday or mountaineering were out of the question.

After years of intense saving and great self-discipline, she was at long last able to afford a trip to the Tegernsee. She met old friends and did a little modest barefoot climbing, for she could not afford boots. Slowly, very slowly, things improved and she went to Berchtesgaden.

When today anyone asks me why one climbs, I should like him to meet Ursula. She is sixty-three years old and could quite easily have become a solitary old lady, embittered by her fate and her loneliness. In actual fact, however, nobody could guess her age. Her capacity for enthusiasm, her resilience and her great interest in life keep her young and attract friends. The way in which she runs her life shows enormous self-control and a capacity for adapting herself to any situation, which she has learned in a hard school, the school of the mountains.

Mountains do not make life easier but they do help to make it easier to bear. Because of the physical conditions, mountains develop one's resistance and give one equanimity. Being in the mountains encourages one to meditate and to find and retain an internal balance which can lead us to the source of practical wisdom.

There are many climbers whose personality has been influenced by mountains, innumerable anonymous climbers who pursue the same aims as myself, with intense enthusiasm. But we do not know them.

We know who first climbed the North Face of the Cima Grande, for their names stand, writ large, like those of Whymper and Carrel, in the annals of Alpine history. We know that Hermann Buhl, after his first solitary ascent of the North-East Face of the Badile, was congratulated by some climbers on the summit. Which route had these unknown climbers ascended? Who were they? Anonymous, unknown climbers.

Countless climbers leave the city every Sunday to make their pilgrimage into the mountains. Their enthusiasm and aims are usually the same as those which inspired Winkler, Preuss, Buhl or Bonatti.

I have met many such climbers, they asked no questions and answered briefly. Only a very few have related their experiences in periodicals. If, during this summer, I have devoted myself in the main to predominantly big climbs and written only about them, that does not mean that the mere rambler is missing something.

The evening sky becomes just as pink for the average climber. His thirst is equally slaked by the fresh spring water and the pines rustle in the breeze for every homeward-bound traveller.

Only enthusiasm and a love of nature are necessary in order to be able to enjoy these delights. The sixth grade does not enter into it. The mountains are just. They take no account of class or difficulty, of size or fluency of speech. They give back to everyone as much as he himself has contributed. They can give more to the rambler than to the conqueror of a 'direttissima'. This depends upon the attitude.

The grade of difficulty does not play a significant role. He who has reached his limit in the third grade, should not try to exceed it. He can gain just as much pleasure from the countless third grade climbs as someone else on an equally large number of sixth-graders. Everybody should recognise what he can and cannot do and adjust his actions accordingly. For this reason the grade of difficulty should above all not be identified with a standard of achievement; it should be possible for one to choose the right way. One must, however, bear in mind that the secret of alpine achievement lies in its limitation – not too high, not too low. Laziness and timidity are not rewarded, the penalty for temerity can be death.

I was certain that Ursula was enjoying this short climb of third or fourth grade as much as I would enjoy a solitary ascent of a sixth grade. My satisfaction over the successful conclusion of the climb seemed to find its counterpart in her as she watched me that afternoon tackle the North-West Ridge of the Torre Grande, alone and without artificial aids. When I got down, a lad approached me and asked me to take him up the Second Tower. There was plenty of time and Ursula, who had engaged me as her guide, had no objection.

The boy, who was about twelve years old, went smartly to work and when we got to the top asked if he would ever be able to do a sixth grade climb. 'Yes,' I said, 'if you train hard and don't get too fat, you'll do it all right.'

An experienced party is often the key to the success of a great climb. I accomplished many of my great first ascents with friends whom I knew and who were as good as I was. I could rely on them and they were always ready to climb again.

Günther, who was a bit short for time this summer, accompanied me up the East Face of the Sassolungo and on the West Face of the Piccola Ciampanide Murfried, and Heini Holzer, with whom I had done many of the most difficult Dolomite climbs, invited me to take part in a first ascent. I also planned to do a climb, which never came off, with Peter Habeler who, after the Andes expedition, had made some sensational first ascents in North America.

Only on one occasion, on Nanga Parbat, did I ever climb with people I didn't know. This experience was a bitter one and in future I will take great care to avoid going on ill-assorted and motley expeditions. I would rather climb alone than with an unknown companion.

However, accompanied by a man like Peter Habeler, I would risk trying an 8000 metre peak, having an equal chance and less risk than when attached to a great expedition with all its customary ballyhoo.

A Handful of Stones

First Ascent of the North-West Face of the Coronelle

As I was tying a bundle of pitons to my harness, my companion, Heini Holzer, picked up a stone from the scree and put it in his pocket. The morning was dull and misty and the rocks were damp and cold.

The North-West Face of the Coronelle lies to the left of the Roda di Vael in the Catinaccio Range and up to now had not been the object of much attention. A grey water channel runs down from the summit and loses itself in yellow overhangs. We had no doubt that the channel in the middle and upper part of the face could be climbed without artificial aids, but how were we going to reach it from below?

I started upwards to the left of the summit fall line over steep rocks and then obliquely to the right to a shallow dièdre. Although the rock was firm and rough, I had to exercise great care, as the soles of my stiff boots threatened to slip on the outward-sloping holds. The rock, for the first few rope lengths, was covered with fine moss and lichen, which were soaked with moisture.

The shallow dièdre, which contained only one tiny hold, made me hesitate. I ascended half a metre and retreated, tried several more times, but without success. My right hand-hold was just large enough to take my finger tips. I had a pressure hold for my left hand on the left wall of the dièdre. In such a situation there is only one way to overcome it.

First of all one takes a good look at the problem, considers the necessary movements and follows them through mentally. Then relax the arms and continue climbing with considerable momentum until larger footholds are available. The secret is that one is always in movement and the impetus thereby achieved is retained until the difficulty is overcome. Less strength is necessary and one can utilise minute holds over short distances. I consider this a much better method than fumbling around, which requires great strength in the fingers and often leads to a fall. Naturally, all this demands much experience and a practised eye. It is frequently the case that rock climbing depends less upon strength than upon the choice of the right route and climbing it in the right manner. This goes for the whole ascent as well as for individual pitches where proper use of the holds and distribution of weight are essential. I would not mind betting that very many climbers have climbed pitches of fifth grade on a fourth grade climb, simply because they were not able to visualise the terrain correctly from below and did not choose the easiest line. This is truer of the lower grades of difficulty than of the sixth grade, as the possibilities decrease with increasing difficulty.

At the next stance, Heini picked up another stone and put it in the pocket of his anorak. We sorted out our equipment here and changed over the lead. Our many climbs together had created a mutual trust in each other and each was aware that the other was no 'kamikaze' climber. The last run-outs led straight over a convex wall to the broken rocks of the summit.

There was a slight drizzle and although the holds were large, we had to hold on tight as the wall was slightly overhanging. We relaxed on the top between three boulders, shared an apple and discussed the descent. Heini fished a handful of stones from his pocket, counted them and threw them over the cliff. As they fell, I counted them and there were seven.

We started down over a slope of broken stones. 'It took seven rope lengths,' said Heini behind me. I turned round. The summit was invisible in the mist.

The South Face of the Marmolata is several kilometres long and about 900 metres in height. It comprises many difficult routes and some of them rank among the most severe in rock climbing.

One of these routes, the Castiglione-Vinatzer Route up the southern precipices of the Marmolata di Rocca, is one of the finest ascents in the Dolomites, at all events in its lower part. On the top half it bears too much to the right and thereby misses the slabby summit pyramid.

I had twice climbed the Castiglione-Vinatzer Route before I thought of making a solo ascent. The first time everything went smoothly and we only took eight hours from start to finish. Günther, my younger brother, was with me. We tried again a year later. We wanted to climb directly to the summit from the shelf which bisects the face by way of the imaginary 'direttissima' which was dictated to us by the mountain. It was not a straight line. I do not like straight lines: the line of a falling drop of water is much too geometric to be beautiful.

We bivouacked in the caves on the shelf and when we crawled out of our tent sack next morning there were twenty centimetres of fresh snow. The memory of our first ascent had gone with the wind. We had to escape from the face as quickly as possible, which we accomplished by following the Livanos Variant.

We left behind fifteen pitons in the middle of the face. We wished to return and try again.

In those days it was becoming increasingly difficult to discover new possibilities for first ascents and when I found one, I was always afraid that somebody else would come along and try to climb it with all the means at their disposal.

It is self-evident that unclimbed routes in the Alps get fewer each year but what is worse is that certain climbers who specialise in first ascents refuse to do anything else and will resort to any sort of artificial aid in order to add to their conquests.

In my opinion, a major first ascent should be 'logical', 'authentic' and 'free', and I always trained diligently in order to meet these requirements.

I started when I was fit and if I was not fit I did not go. Up to date none of my numerous first ascents has been repeated in less time or with less pitons than I originally used and that is very gratifying.

Finger Exercises by a Potential Suicide

First Solo Ascent of the South Face Direct of the
Marmolata di Rocca

One morning when I went to fetch my car it was not there. At the
mill, where it ought to have been, the grass was pressed down and
I thought I detected a track leading away in the direction of the
street.

I had returned from a trip late the night before and had locked
the car. In order to use both hands to lock the door, I had put my
briefcase containing all my papers and unanswered mail on the
roof. I was quite positive about all this.

The police were not very helpful: 'Sometimes we get them back,
sometimes we don't. We'll have to wait and see.'

I was thus confined to my attic and could only get to the practice
rocks, which were five minutes outside the town.

Whenever I came into my room, I got out a photo of the South
Face of the Marmolata and studied it with care. The enormous
grey flight of slabs above the shelf was intersected by a number of
shallow cracks. There were also niches and cavities in profusion
and one crack appeared to lead directly to the summit of the Punta
di Rocca. The photo was taken by Jürgen Winkler; he made pictures which can be studied with a magnifying glass.

I spent my days either in my room or at the old saw-mill. The
more I trained, the more I toyed with the idea of climbing the
route on the Marmolata di Rocca alone. I asked several climbers
for their opinion and whether they would join me, but they all
considered it impossible.

A crack runs up the lower part of the South Face of the Marmolata di Rocca.
This crack constitutes the Castiglione-Vinatzer Route. Reinhold Messner
climbed alone up the series of slabs above the ledge direct to the
summit. Some of those who tried to repeat this route were forced
to retreat.

This route was my own idea, I had reviewed it from A to Z and had trained for it for a long time.

I would need two days; for many hours I would have to wriggle up small cracks, straddle up wide dièdres and balance my way up smooth slabs. The descent should take me about an hour. Strange thoughts circulated in my brain, I had become a fanatic, I already lived on the face without even having started.

Next day I went back to the police station. The sergeant referred to his big filing index of stolen cars; mine was not there, it was in the other one – 'Cars Found'. While he was on the telephone I began playing with a small spring which I kept in my jacket pocket for finger exercises. He saw this, laughed and asked me what was the object of the exercise. When I told him, he said, 'Very dangerous, you are a potential suicide.'

Many people regard mountaineering as being equivalent to death and for that reason are against it. I used to tell them that motoring is much more dangerous, but they just did not understand.

When I got my car back about half an hour later, I should have liked to start off for the Marmolata at once, but it was too late, so I went home and packed my rucksack.

Next morning I was really ready to start. My mother was not alarmed when I told her that I was going off on my own to the Marmolata for a few days. 'Be very careful,' she said, as always.

I spent the night in the bivouac hut on the Ombretta Pass. As it was cold in the early morning and I did not feel much like climbing, I made a late start. I knew the Vinatzer Route so well from previous ascents that I had no need to look for the way. I did not find it any more difficult than I remembered it from previous years.

I found a bivouac site in one of the cavities on the ledge and settled myself in. There was water close by which I mixed with lemon squash. I found last year's pitons and hung them with the others on my harness. I settled down early, it was dark outside the cave and the air began to get cold. I drew up my legs and put my head inside the bivouac sack.

When dawn broke, I had no desire to get up. It is impossible to ignore or even curtail this hour, this period, when one lies apathetic and cold. During the night, when I lay half asleep, I kept thinking that I might not be able to make my way direct to the summit. I was aware of these moments of doubt and was able to brush them aside.

A fly sat on my sack, rubbing its legs together, first the front legs and then the back ones. It rubbed them together in pairs and appeared to enjoy it. When the fly had gone, I roused myself, massaged my arms and legs and got up.

Then I stowed all my gear in my rucksack, fastened on my harness and checked that the pitons were hanging from the right karabiners. I always arranged them in order of size and section, so that they were ready to hand in an emergency. I fastened both étriers together and attached them to my back by means of a karabiner. Some ten metres from the cave I hammered a channel piton into the overhang. Belayed in this way, I left the shelf and ascended a steep pitch. Higher up, the wall receded somewhat and I climbed straight up over a succession of slabs, jagged rocks and a loose convex bulge, without having to insert more pitons.

I was relieved to find that the going was more easy than I had expected. I rested for a moment below a vertical step. The holds were so far apart that further progress looked too difficult. Further to the left, however, I thought I could detect a half-hidden fissure which seemed promising. I traversed to the left over organ pipe-shaped rock pillars and saw a narrow crack at the back of a small dièdre. The rock above the crack was vertical and brittle but the piton which I drove into the crack held firm. A spell of extremely strenuous climbing enabled me to surmount the pitch, belayed by three pitons, and I was home and dry.

This was one of the most difficult pitches which I have ever climbed; after a short breather, I sweated up a long slab. Whenever I was faced with a difficult situation I looked around for firmer holds – and always found them. 'This isn't right,' I would say to myself when I began to feel insecure, then I thought for a moment, changed a hand- or foot-hold and continued on my way. It was not until I had climbed a series of cracks and grooves that I realised that the sky had become overcast and hail was beginning to fall.

I now left the direct line and made towards a crack which led to the right-hand arête, just below the summit. I reached the crack after a pitch of very severe free climbing and pegged my way up it for some twenty metres or so. The rope ran through the karabiner and I climbed as though in a roped party, except that I manipulated the rope myself. When I was able to resort to free climbing once more, I hammered in two abseil pitons, climbed down and retrieved the karabiner. I left the pitons, as I no longer had any use for them. Very pleased with myself, I ascended the last few steps to the summit.

This first ascent will perhaps always continue to be one of my most important climbs. The reason for this is that it so admirably corresponded to the nature of the mountain and the classic quality of the 'direttissima'. I spent two days on this face, I had held on to it by my finger tips and explored its surface. I never calculated – I considered and observed.

I do not regard a mountain just as a mass of stone, but as an organism, which one observes and with which one lives.

In the beginning there were no routes on mountains, they came when man had conceived them, thought over them and climbed them. These routes are not indispensable, but possible, and that which, generally speaking, applies to created objects is also applicable to a first ascent.

It rained almost without stopping on the homeward journey from East Tyrol. There was a large number of dead frogs on the road, a sign of bad weather.

Sepp Mayerl had organised a climbers' meet in the Lienz Dolomites; we climbed the Laserz Ridge and discussed future problems in the mountains of the world.

I still had a lot of plans for the rest of the summer. I had acquired some good light equipment and all that was missing was the necessary stimulus and a suitable companion. My condition, that is to say my psycho-physical condition, had suffered less from aggressive critics than from the fact that I had succeeded in making a solo ascent of the Marmolata 'direttissima'.

The tension which this face built up in me before the climb made me utilise every minute of training to the full and often during the climb itself I found my thoughts concentrating on isolated difficult pitches. This complete absorption with the problem was rather like a yoga exercise and put me in the necessary psycho-physical frame of mind to enable me to bring this first ascent to a successful conclusion.

Now, however, I no longer had an objective on which I could concentrate all my strength and energy. Within a few weeks I had become uncertain of myself and abandoned a number of routes without having been under serious pressure. It was not until a month later that I found my old form again.

The Great Wall

Thirty metres below the exit crack I was suddenly overcome by fear. I had forgotten to bring along any wooden wedges and the crack, which was about five centimetres wide, was smooth and overhanging.

I had previously been climbing on the Marmolata, the Civetta, Les Droites and the Frêney Pillar – in fact where had I not been that summer! I thus found it hard to comprehend that things were not working out well and that the confidence which I had built up during these climbs had evaporated, leaving behind a sense of fear which prevented me from tackling this last impasse. I had no desire to go down and climb the whole route over again. Irresolute, I stood for more than an hour at the bottom of the crack until I finally made up my mind to retreat.

Hans Frisch, a first-rate climber from Bruneck, formerly a climbing companion of Toni Egger and a fearless solo exponent, was in agreement provided we tried again during the course of the next few days. A short time ago we had succeeded in making the first ascent of the North-East Buttress of the Gardenaccia and during the descent into the Badia Valley we became intrigued by the huge slab system on the Monte Cavallo which lay opposite us, bathed in the evening light. It looked very tempting. To the right of the three prominent buttresses rises an immense compact wall bisected by a ledge. A series of narrow cracks indicated the route, which we forthwith dubbed the 'Great Wall'.

The Monte Cavallo above the Badia Valley in the Dolomites.
To the left, the Livanos Buttress, then the Central Buttress and the
Right-hand Buttress. The 'Great Wall' lies to the right.

So now I was frustrated just a rope's length below the summit. I drove in two pitons, looped them together with line, threaded through the rope and began the descent. We slid down on the doubled rope past all the terrain over which we had so hopefully ascended a few hours before. We frequently swung free in the air, spinning round and round, so that we were forced to shut our eyes in order not to become dizzy.

Some days later, we went once more into the Badia Valley, *en route* for the Monte Cavallo. I had got my confidence back and although I realised that the difficulty which had stopped us on the uncompleted climb remained the same, we started up. Confidence is often stronger than discernment.

In the meantime I had neither trained nor climbed, time had passed me by without my being aware of it. At that time I no longer had a sense of time, none of my previous summers had seemed to last so long, time had stood still.

I had regained my form as rapidly as I had lost it. The numerous expeditions, the frequently recurring difficult situations, meeting other men, had all made me very tired but otherwise unchanged.

We had at last reached the shelf via broken rocks and some steep pitches. Above us loomed the main difficulty: a large overhang. Some of the pitons used on the last attempt were still *in situ* but this time I was able to do with fewer. The big overlapping rock was still attached to the wall and once again I treated it with extreme caution. It was very large, about six metres square, and looked as though it might break away at any moment. At this point we traversed to the right into a system of shallow grooves, by means of which we reached the final exit crack. Once again I stood below the narrow crevice, but this time however I had the necessary wooden wedges hanging from my harness. But I did not have to use them, for I was able to hammer some pitons into existing holes to the right and left of the crack, which constituted an excellent belay. The greater portion of the crack I climbed free. I left the unused wedges behind on the summit.

The Maestri Route on the Roda di Vael in the Catinaccio is one of the many artificial climbs which have become increasingly popular during the last few years. It is about 400 metres in height and largely overhanging. It is by no means in the same category as a sixth grade climb but, from the technical point of view, it is not easy. At the same time this type of climbing is hard on the arms and one gets fed up with the beastly pitons.

If I were to have faith in the further development of mountaineering with the increasing use of artificial aids, then I would consider the Maestri Route as one of the landmarks in alpine history. But I do not have that faith and for that reason I was rather amused to see so many pitons on such a small face.

Anyone wishing to encounter the imaginary seventh grade must look elsewhere. If perhaps once a year I have been induced to tackle an artificial climb, it is only so that I do not entirely lose my piton technique.

Once A Year

Below us lay the cirque. Nothing was moving there. The pitons above us protruded from the rotten rock at regular intervals. Rusty iron in ridiculous positions.

On the previous evening an Italian climber was waiting for me at home. He wanted at all costs to be taken on a climb: when was unimportant, but it must be with me and it must be the Maestri Route on the Roda di Vael.

For some days I had avoided coming in contact with climbers who might ask questions about my plans. If I had really given expression to my dreams, I might have been forced to disclose plans which would have startled even my friends.

He therefore complied with my wishes and we talked about artificial climbing instead of free climbs in the Dolomites.

Until recently I had never taken part in an artificial climb, I had held aloof from them as I did not want to waste my time.

For some hours I had been standing on the middle rungs of étriers. With mixed feelings I tested the loose pitons, which many others must have done before me. Karabiners hung clinking from a sling. The rope, hanging down between my legs, looked rather like a spider clinging to the rocks. After each run-out I tied myself on tight and, sitting in slings, was able to belay with ease. When it was time for me to go on, I stood in the étriers and waited until my companion was attached to at least two pitons.

I hammered in the loose pitons and if one seemed ready to come out under my weight, I cautiously took my weight off it. All these somewhat chancy manoeuvres were very complicated. After some time we had, so to speak, 'played ourselves in' and I became adept at pulling out the pitons.

Late that afternoon as I was occupied with the last great overhang, many small details which I had forgotten came back to me, such as tiny shells in crevices of the rock, lichens, a wall-creeper bird.

Our climb terminated about seven o'clock in the evening.

Our somewhat tattered attire, our lacerated fingers, pitons and coils of rope must have presented a picture of a party tired enough to demand a respite from their labours.

A trifle bemused, we sorted out our equipment which was in rather a chaotic state after our manoeuvres at the great overhang.

There are climbers who maintain that it is only by good luck that I am still alive and they are right. Who is not however? A car accident, a falling stone, an avalanche, a severe illness . . . It is a fact, on the other hand, that not even the best luck in the world would have been of any use without my experience and endurance.

It is possible to make a theoretical calculation as to how long one can go on climbing until one eventually falls off. To my mind there is not much danger in doing a difficult route alone, if it is within one's capacity. The fault lies with those who do not know when to stop, who are always on the search for fresh difficulties and climb on regardless of the time.

The Soldà Route on the Sassolungo is one of the most difficult on the mountain and the longest. In addition to which it was seldom done and these factors tempted me to climb it alone.

The South-West Face of the Marmolata, which Gino Soldà climbed for the first time a few days after his Sassolungo route, has become celebrated. Hermann Buhl and Kuno Rainer have climbed it in winter and Cesare Maestri has done it solo. It is now done three or four times a year.

The Sassolungo Route, on the other hand, has been neglected. Since 1936, the number of ascents can be counted on the fingers of one hand.

When I asked Gino Soldà which of his routes was his favourite, he said the North Face Direct on the Sassolungo, for the following reasons:

'It combines length and difficulty. There is no escape from it in rain or snow. It is the type of climb which above a certain height makes either ascent or descent appear impossible.'

No Way Out

First Solo Ascent of the Soldà Route on the North Face
of the Sassolungo

Once more I stood below the North Face of the Sassolungo but I
still was not sure if I should start. I had been there three times
that summer and three times I had gone away.

'I should have started this morning,' I said to myself.

Every time I passed through the Gardena Valley to the Sella
Pass I was compelled to look up at this mighty and symmetrical
wall. Over the years since my first great climbs, I had often thought
of the buttress which forms the right-hand edge of the face and
rises from the woods to the summit in two parts. I had often toyed
with the idea of creating a new route there.

During the course of the last few weeks I had come here with
the intention of seeking out the Soldà Route, which is not accurately described in any climbing guide.

Now I was here again. I clambered up the vast scree slopes to
the start. It was already past midday and I was in a hurry. Whenever I had to stop for breath, I gazed up at the wall. The peak
towered above its massive wide base. I was too close and the view
was too foreshortened for me to take it all in. I could now discern
some cracks and shelves, which did not appear to increase the
possibilities. A waterfall rushed down the great central couloir.
Every now and then small stones plunged down into the hard
snow which spread out like a large cone at the bottom of the
couloir. Instinctively I settled my helmet more firmly on my head.
I was carrying the rope on my back.

It became easier after two pitches. By way of a ramp I reached a slab, which I had to cross in order to get into a deep gully. I took the rope off my back and, having added a second piton to the one *in situ*, tied a sling to them and threaded through the rope. Belayed in this manner, I ascended obliquely upwards to the right. Here I drove in another piton and swung down on the rope into the great couloir. Then I drew in the rope, thus cutting off my retreat. I relied too much on my strength and had no thought of what might happen. I left the couloir by the right-hand wall and soon came up against extreme difficulties. I was forced to climb on wet and splintered rock. Up to now everything had been firm but I no longer felt quite so sure of myself. With great care I took a piton off the karabiner on my harness and managed to drive it in a few centimetres with a few blows of the hammer. I was standing on small footholds and the hold for my left hand was so wet that I had to work quickly. I hammered hard on the iron spike, when suddenly there was a loud crack – the shaft had broken off, but fortunately some fibres of wood still remained attached to the head.

I was at first unable to take in the significance of this event. Above and below were vertical rocks.

I was on the Sassolungo, on the Soldà Route on the North Face, in a wet and difficult crack, 700 metres above the cirque.

Having considered all this, I endeavoured to continue without artificial aids or belay. My intention was to climb in such a manner that if necessary I could always retreat to the last holds. I did not get very far and after one or two steps I had to come down.

I was now really up against it, it was no go. I had already tried twice to climb up from the piton, but in vain. I would have to drive the piton right in in order to get a belay. If I could do this it would be easier higher up. I held the stump of the hammer between finger and thumb and tried to knock it in. 'Made in Italy' was stamped on it. The rest of the shaft hung useless from the red cord which was much too thick. I could use it as an abseil loop if the piton holds, I thought. It wouldn't go in. I was sweating all over, especially my fingers – I was afraid.

'I shall have to call for help,' I said to myself. For the first time in my life I had to consider this possibility. But who could hear me? A shepherd perhaps, or a rambler. It was late afternoon, would there be anybody there, at the foot of the wall?

At the start I had only feared objective dangers but I had overcome this fear as I climbed.

Suddenly there was no way out but I could not give up. I also could not go on standing there for hours. The more absurd a situation is, the less bearable is the thought of death. I had to do something before it was too late. For the first time I realised the value of a piton hammer.

Great difficulties lay behind me and possibly still greater ones ahead. I had sought them and now would be glad if only I could escape from the trap. Owing to my precarious stance, I had to do my utmost to get away from it. With extreme caution I wormed myself upwards, looking ahead for small stances. I climbed slowly from ledge to ledge, fully realising that if this did not work, I should have to go back. It was easier to continue upwards than down. I was so keyed up that I was oblivious to everything around me.

Gradually the face receded a little and I was able to find a stance on a platform about as big as a chair. I leaned my head against the wall and closed my eyes. Slowly I began to forget where I was, forgot the broken hammer. Strange shapes rose up before me, faces, staring and motionless. When I opened my eyes again, I saw the grey Dolomite wall with fine moss lying in the cracks. The irregularities of the rock stood out, clear and lustrous, they became interwoven with the moss, forming fantastic pictures. Moments later these images faded away and merged into a grey billowy substance and, when I could see clearly again, the rock had returned.

Beneath me in the depths of the narrow, dark couloir, a stone or fragment of ice fell noisily, leaping from one side to the other. Minutes passed before all was silent again. The trees down in the cirque looked like toys, their needles gleaming in the sun. To the left and right the two buttresses soared upwards, yellow and overhanging, and, when I remembered that the wall below me was five times as high, I clung all the more firmly to my holds.

All was quiet now, everything around was as before: the cirque, the walls and gullies. There they lay, neutral and indifferent, as though man had never existed.

The exit crack was blocked by a huge overhang, which, rather surprisingly, I was able to circumvent with comparative ease. Much relieved, I reached easier ground and after ascending an icy couloir and some broken rocks, I got to the top in the early hours of the evening.

I was completely exhausted and sat down for a rest. My whole body was tense. I was too fatigued to sleep, I just sat there and noticed that my hands were trembling.

One can only fall off once, I thought, never a second time. Perhaps I was able to understand, at least momentarily, what 'never a second time' meant. That night as I stumbled down from the gap above the Sassolungo Cirque to the Sella Pass, I reflected that everything would be the same even if I were not there and I felt that there was something that I still had to learn: to laugh at myself.

It was about this time that I got a letter containing the following criticism: 'You're a madman, a real nut-case – soon to become a child of death, if you cannot find the strength and courage combined with reason to give up such ventures.'

I was well aware that many others looked upon my solitary climbs as irresponsible. They were regarded as an ultimate peril which lay beyond the scope of everyday life. I had even been reproached for being responsible for those who had been killed whilst attempting to repeat my routes. If however, I am to be represented as a potential danger, one should not ignore the long and intensive training which I have undergone. Someone like myself, who has conscientiously trained and has twenty years of climbing experience behind him, is probably exposed to less risk on a severe solo climb than the man who rapidly embarks on a week-end expedition without being particularly fit.

There were also some people who expressed doubts about some of my solo ascents; for example, they said that I had never done Les Droites Face. The French climbers, who had watched my progress on the face almost uninterruptedly, wrote about this expedition as follows: 'There is no doubt that this is the most severe solo ascent in mixed terrain which has been carried out in the Western Alps since the Second World War.'

I went on with my solitary climbing not in order to do something more difficult but solely because I had the necessary qualifications and plenty of time.

Sixth grade in the Himalayas. In order to make this very severe pitch on the South Face of Manaslu practicable for the Sherpas, it had to be made safe with fixed ropes and ladders.

When a Spoon Falls from the Table

Second Ascent (First Solo Ascent) of the Meran Route
on the North Face of the Furchetta

Cautiously I inserted a 'knife-blade' piton into the crack and with
my other hand pulled the hammer from its pouch on my harness
and tapped it gently on the top. It held, but when I gave it a hefty
blow it sprang out and shot past my head down the cliff. I started
back involuntarily while the iron spike went clattering down in
huge bounds.

I had just made a traverse obliquely upwards to the right, using
wooden wedges, and this piton would have enabled me to reach
easier ground.

There was no point in shedding tears over the hard piton or the
unyielding crack in the wall; if I wanted to go on, I had to drive in
another piton and do it quickly. I smelled danger in the air, the
danger of coming off.

The deep conviction of the ever-present danger of falling should
not inhibit the solitary climber. Ease of movement and complete
detachment can only occur if the climber identifies himself with
the individual pitch and abandons himself to the magic of the
moment. The ability to concentrate works right down to the
fingers and soles of the boots which cling to the rocks.

I frequently got so absorbed at difficult pitches that I became
quite oblivious of time. I thought about all manner of subjects,
except one, death.

I thought, I felt, that my life would continue indefinitely. Of
course, when I thought more deeply about it, I realised that I must
die sometime, but this was in the distant future and had no

The North Face of the Furchetta seen from the Munkel path.
The Meran Route runs up the huge dièdre on the right-hand side of the
wall; an excellent climb.

substance. Other things claimed priority: life, this piton, this expedition.

I was ready for anything, because I had faith that I would survive.

I was well aware of the fear of bodily and spiritual failure at the decisive moment, the fear of objective dangers. But not fear of death. Not because I regarded myself as brave, but because death just did not enter into my calculations.

In the meantime, I had driven in another piton, tied on this time. Again it sprang out and again I was startled.

If a spoon falls from the table, you bend down and pick it up. That is an everyday occurrence and nobody is alarmed.

On a steep face however, far above the cirque, it is quite another matter. A clattering piton, a falling stone or a dive-bombing chough make one aware for a moment of the gaping abyss, the vertiginous depths. For a fraction of a second one subconsciously identifies oneself with the falling object. The act of falling takes on a new significance. I have discovered that experienced mountaineers, who treat a severe climb almost as a matter of course, when they are off their guard at home in normal surroundings become startled out of all proportion if something falls to the ground.

Having surmounted this artificial pitch, I made rapid progress and, joining the arête on the right, I followed it until it merged into a yellow buttress. I now made a traverse which involved some abseiling over to the Solleder Route, which at this point unites with the Meran Route.

Here I took off the rope which I had been using as a belay from time to time and tied it on my back French fashion.

I was climbing this part of the wall for the fourth time and when I reflected that this was the first sixth grade climb in the Dolomites, I was amazed how far the sixth grade had developed since that time.

After Angelo Dibona, Hans Dülfer and Luis Trenker had made an attempt on the Furchetta North Face. They too were forced to retreat, just below what is known today as the Dülfer Pulpit. Ten years later, Emil Solleder could not get any further and discovered this series of cracks over to the right which lead up to the summit roof.

I was now situated just below the overhanging roof and was uncertain whether I should belay myself or not. Three years previously, on the occasion of the first winter ascent, we did not use pitons and the rocks were cold and covered with snow. I was in much better form now and the face was dry and pleasantly warm. I decided against the rope. I wormed my way up the narrow crack and reached the icy terminal chimney.

As I was writing my name in the summit book, I considered the possibility of a solo ascent of the Vinatzer Route which would undoubtedly demand an abundance of expertise and courage.

Hans Vinatzer continued the Direct Route up to the summit from the spot where Dülfer and Solleder had failed, thereby demonstrating that there is no absolute limit in rock climbing. He was many years ahead of his time and must have undergone intensive training to be able to climb a severe face of this nature without ever having to consider the possibility of coming off.

I could have stayed at home and sunbathed, instead of which I was lying at the bottom of the South-East Face of the Scotoni. This morning I could not make up my mind to start and now it was too late.

Six months had passed since the Andes expedition and my momentum had evaporated. I had expected to reach my best form in the spring, but now I was forced to admit that I was tired. Owing to the manner in which I had carried on my training in steps – from the six thousanders of the Andes to the four thousanders of the Alps and the three thousanders of the Dolomites – I had attained a high-spot in free climbing in the course of a month and this had now just as rapidly faded away. Training was not much more use, I was overtrained and, moreover, my attitude towards big climbs had changed.

When I arrived at the start of a climb, I no longer had an inferiority complex, I had climbed every face at least once and I knew that I could reach the summit within a few hours.

I longed to recover that feeling of reverential awe, I would have liked to regard the mountains again with the eyes of a novice.

Every man has his dreams, especially the young mountaineer. Sooner or later he seeks to turn these dreams into reality, for he cannot live with a dream which does not materialise. He tries, therefore, to make it come true.

I had not got any further with my plans, much less brought them to a successful conclusion. The 'seventh grade' had no place in my dreams at that time. I was neither fascinated by it nor was it an objective.

Climbing the North-East Face Direct on the Sassolungo. The Gardena Valley lies far below in the sunshine. It was icy cold on the face.

It Would Have Been Dry in Summer

First Ascent of the North-East Face Direct of the Sassolungo

The early snows had melted in the cirque so we decided to start. Dark strips of black ice standing out from the grey rock marked the cracks and gullies to be avoided. Further up small snow patches indicated the general line of our proposed ascent. It led for more than 1000 metres up the vertical wall direct to the summit.

Both creativity and self-possession are necessary in opening up a route. The undefined boundary between enthusiasm and ecstasy in many climbers is attributable to this and I frequently ask myself why so many of them place such little importance on stylishness in their routes.

The great Dolomite faces, the Civetta, the Marmolata and Monte Agnèr, had always fascinated me. This summer I had discovered the North Face of the Sassolungo and had climbed several routes on it. A wall 1000 metres high poses quite a different problem from one of only 500 and as one must be especially competent to cope with difficulties at greater heights, the highest cliffs will provide even more difficult climbs than those already completed. I am certain that the so-called seventh grade has already been achieved in many a practice area. There, however, it is of little value. I am also convinced that the Elbe Sandstone Mountains, which actually have a seventh grade, present difficulties which far exceed those of our sixth grade. Here, however, we are only dealing with practice routes a few rope lengths in height at the most. The 'seventh grade' on a great face, on the other hand, with its isolation and solitude, provides one of the possibilities of further development in classical alpine climbing.

Naturally I know that at the moment it is not possible to overcome such difficulties on the great faces of the earth, on 8000 metre peaks, but I am equally convinced that they will be solved on alpine walls.

Just as very severe Himalayan mountaineering will develop in such a manner that a single roped party will be able to overcome an 8000-metre face without the use of oxygen or extraneous aids, so it will become the wish of some young climbers to master the difficulties on the great alpine faces without recourse to expansion bolts and other such devices.

I first became aware of this new line on the North Face of the Sassolungo on the occasion of my solitary ascent of the Soldà Route. It goes straight up to the summit through a couloir, followed by a series of cracks and a barely-defined rock buttress between the Soldà Route to the left and the main route to the right.

Dawn had scarcely broken as we started. The avalanche cone at the foot was full of holes caused by falling stones. This morning, however, the face was quiet as they were held in place by the frost. Only once in the course of the morning did we hear a rattle from far above but it died away in another couloir.

With incredible slowness, which almost drove us to despair, we arrived at the buttress above the couloir. We tried to avoid the ice but in vain, we met it in every crack, on the holds and stances. There was not a vestige of sunshine, there did not appear to be any life on this face. Not even the choughs came to visit it. For a north face, the rock was surprisingly firm. This was probably because sunless north faces weather more slowly than their southern counterparts.

It was just about two o'clock in the afternoon when we finally reached some broken rocks but the first autumn snow, icy and clear, lay in the deep cracks.

Without undue haste, as we were only about 300 metres from the top, I swung over into a gully, belayed by Sepp. I cut tiny notches in the ice with my piton hammer and worked my way upwards. The end of the gully terminated in a chimney with ice-clad walls up which I forced my way. I stopped after a couple of metres, seized by an uncanny feeling of insecurity and inexplicable doubts about the way ahead. My lips were split by the cold and my fingers were sore from cutting so many steps with the hammer. Despite this, however, I was sustained by the certainty that we would reach the summit today.

Cautiously I roped down on the stiff ropes to Sepp Mayerl. He was marking time on the stance as his toes were hurting. He had got frostbite in the Andes and had only recently recovered. The pain was so great that he was obliged to kick his feet against the rocks every few minutes.

Furious over the bad conditions, we stood still for a time and debated whether we should retreat and abseil down to the bottom. Sepp wanted to continue and leaned back in order to judge whether the ridge was climbable or not. It proved difficult but we did it.

Sepp Mayerl is one of those few climbers who always gets there. He is not a specialist, he is equally as good on rock as on ice. He owes this all-round skill to the fact that he built up his experience step by step over the years.

Under normal conditions this part of the wall would not have presented any difficulty, in fact we probably would have climbed it unroped. If we had not found an abseil piton just where it reared up vertically, we might have had to bivouac.

I ascended a fragmented pitch which was clear of snow, but my fingers were stiff and frozen to the bone. We finally climbed up a snowy gully and reached the summit.

'We had to fight our way up like a winter ascent,' I said on the way down, but Sepp simply remarked wrily, 'It would have been dry in summer.'

In addition to enjoying a great summer in the mountains, I received an invitation to a climbers' meet in Trento, an annual event under the auspices of the International Film Festival.

After reporting to the office, pleased with the invitation but at the same time depressed that I was missing my climbing in this glorious weather, I saw the first film. It was nothing to write home about.

We spent the evening in the 'Cantinotta', a well-known tavern in the old town. A number of important people were there. It was a great honour to be there with them, but it got a bit boring. All one heard were accounts of summer, expeditions but only fragments; most of them had done some big climbs, as might be expected, and everyone was pleased that he had made the best of the summer. They were all shaking hands, patting each other on the back and congratulating one another over this or that first ascent.

Later on in the street with a few friends, we met Pierre who had just turned up and we all suddenly realised that he had been missing up to now. We all went back to the bar at Pierre's insistence, irrespective of closing hours.

Next morning the principal item on the programme was a round-table conference on 'Women in the Mountains'. A journalist had reserved a seat for me in the great hall which was teeming with women.

Woman is equal to man in the mountains, in fact, superior. This was the general theme as I understood it and it all went to prove that woman – despite a remark to the contrary attributed to the great Paul Preuss – is not 'the ruination of mountaineering'. This statement is not entirely easy to prove, so I turned it round and said that it should really mean 'Mountains are the ruination of women'. This caused a furore, they all leapt out of their seats ranting and raving. I did not

138

go so far as to ask them if they could prove that this was not the case – that would have been a bit too much.

All this excitement was not in the least necessary. What the women wanted to hear was that they could pull their weight in the mountains and that they were the equal of men, Women's Lib. and all that. The speakers did their best to mollify them, so that the discussion became a little one-sided. Until I threw a spanner into the works, everything in the garden was lovely, one hymn of praise to the world of women after another. Who would have expected anything else?

There are women mountaineers who are excellent climbers, there are some who are even better than men and there is a select body which can lead climbs of the sixth grade.

When I somewhat arrogantly said something about 'aping the prerogative of men', I really set the cat among the pigeons. This was going too far, so I was cast forth from the alpine world of women. Everybody in the hall talked at once, nobody understood anything and quite a few got really worked up. One or two approached me and tapped me on the chest with outstretched forefinger. However, I took all this in my stride.

Five Climbs in a Day

An autumnal wind was blowing on the Stripsenjoch, there were a lot of ramblers about but very few climbers. As Walter Troi and I started up the Dülfer Route on the Fleischbank, Günther, with some friends from the Villnöss section of the Italian Alpine Club, strolled over to the West Face of the Predigtstuhl. We were glad to participate in this joint venture in the Kaisergebirge and had promised to take the most active members of our club up one or other of the peaks.

The rock was more sound here than in the Dolomites but the holds, on the other hand, were so greasy that the climbing could easily be hazardous. During the summer I had developed a fine sense of friction climbing, but now this did not work any more and I clung tightly to all the holds. There were so many pitons in the Spiral Crack that one could have climbed it artificially. However, if one is going to desist from using pitons as a means of progression a popular route would get more difficult year by year.

Whenever I came to a new district I invariably repeated routes of medium difficulty in order to become acquainted with the terrain and the type of rock. I did not attempt any severe climbs or first ascents until I had mastered all this.

We had great fun on the traverse of the Fleischbank East Face but the terminal chimney proved very tricky.

I climbed the Christaturm Ridge alone after coming down from the Fleischbank summit and found it rather dangerous. I had neither rope nor karabiner and found the worn and greasy holds unpleasant.

When I got to the top I decided that I would do no more solo climbs on such worn rock. I met Günther at the bottom, he had just come down from the Predigtstuhl and we went up it again together. We again chose one of the Dülfer routes and, as we climbed, we talked about this pioneer of the Kaisergebirge. We were both very interested in alpine history and often climbed certain routes solely from historical considerations. In our opinion, this formed part of the all-round education of a mountaineer.

On our next climb, the North Arête of the Goinger Halt, we overtook other parties. We were not roped and reached the summit in a few minutes. As we still had time for a fifth climb, we decided to do the Rittler Ridge on the Bauernpredigtstuhl, which still had the afternoon sun on it. We chose the Rebitsch Variant via the overhang and higher up we got on to the main Rebitsch Route by chance. The rock here was good and climbing a joy. I got held up once at a rock bulge but I discovered an old rusty piton which indicated that we were still on the correct route.

It was an autumn day in November, I had not climbed for some time and had lost that fatigue which comes from excess energy.

Now, in the autumn, it seemed as though summer had never been. When I left the shady side streets and the neon-lit lecture halls, I stopped and enjoyed the warm sun on the bridge. I looked over the rooftops at the Catinaccio which had a slight sprinkling of snow and would be soon in shadow. Noise welled up from the dusty streets but the river below me ran silently. I thought of the North Face of the Second Sella Tower; I wanted to do a climb before the winter set in, a short, difficult and delicate rock ascent. I considered the North-West Face Direct on the Second Sella Tower, of which I made the first ascent last summer. I remembered it was free climbing on iron-hard rock and was aware that some of those who tried to repeat it had afiled. I was attracted by the idea of trying it alone.

As a rule, it is not usual to climb a very severe route twice of which one has made the first ascent. The North-West Face Direct on the Second Tower, however, is incomparable and is one of those climbs which one would like to do again.

The Black Dot on the Wall

'You've got to be lucky,' I said as I strode about the classroom. I had not yet got used to the fixed hours and felt a bit strange.

All heads turned towards me, curious and interrogatory. So I told them a story, as I often did when the mathematics lesson was concluded ahead of time and the students were restless.

'Yesterday,' I began and looked out of the window into the November rain. The students did not know that it was already snowing in the mountains.

'Yesterday,' I began again, 'my summer ended.' I had completed a last climb on the Sella Towers.

Suddenly everybody noticed a black dot on the North-West Face Direct on the Second Tower, apparently a man whom nobody knew and who had not left his name at the hut, let alone his rucksack. All one knew about this dot was that it was moving and might fall off at any moment. It was late afternoon and there was great excitement at the foot of the face. I was standing on a small ledge about three rope lengths up, when someone shouted from below, 'I can see him too now.'

The sun was low over the Sasso Levante, a fiery ball in the sky illuminating the fresh snow. It sent its last warm rays onto the North Face as though it wanted to help this man out of the dilemma in which he apparently found himself. The light shone benevolently on the smooth grey rock wall, even the dark wet streaks of water took on a friendly aspect and now and again something glinted up aloft like a reflection from a metal object.

'That'll be the karabiners,' said someone suddenly, who apparently knew something about climbing. And then there was the white helmet – there was no doubt that it was a man, almost certainly a climber. I was standing level with the ledge leading from the Third Tower, opposite was the Sassolungo, already in shadow, the peaks of the Geisler Group shrouded in mist, sunset . . . Only the North Face of the Second Tower was clear – he must have been making for it and had lost the route.

They might not have seen him for a long time, perhaps never, if a party which had had to turn back had not paused below the North Face, just as he started a stone falling, inadvertently, I think. At all events, it startled those below and they looked up the wall. As they connected the falling stone with the black dot on the face, they dropped their sacks and one of them got out his binoculars and relayed a hair-raising description of what he saw. They were soon in shadow, as the sun was sinking and twilight was rapidly approaching, slowly but surely.

This advent of twilight is one of the most tranquil hours on a mountain. It is at its best, I find, just below the summit on a north face and one emerges as the sun is going down.

Meanwhile the spectators had increased in number. For a long time there was no movement from the black dot. The know-alls down below on the path were of the opinion that the mountain rescue service should be informed, for they were all convinced that it must be a climber who had got stuck and could neither climb up nor down. The spectators, it would appear, wanted him rescued.

The climber was undoubtedly still at the same spot. The less he moved – and I cannot rid myself of the impression that he was waiting on purpose – the more the tension rose down below. The sun had gone down, even the North Face lay in shadow; now at last something must happen even if it had nothing to do with the climber, who for the last hour had seemed unperturbed. (Otherwise surely he would have called for help.) He moved his hands over the wall above him, plainly visible through the binoculars, and was apparently oblivious of the fact that if he came off he would fall straight down to the cirque below. But he did not and the spectators had wasted their time, so, talking animatedly to one another, they left the scene.

Then suddenly, without warning, he started to move. Slowly but decisively, now that the others had lost patience, he began to climb. Legs wide apart, quite quietly without wasting much time looking for holds, he climbed straight up through a narrow chimney.

He did not go very far, once more he came to a standstill below an overhang, his legs wide apart and feeling the wall with his hands. It seemed as though he was looking for holds. He maintained the same position; it almost seemed as though he had become part of the rock. Only when he moved was it certain that he was alive.

Night had fallen now and all the spectators had vanished, but I was in no hurry. Oblivious of everything around me, I let the night take its course. I should have liked to go down but I could not have descended for more than a few metres. I started up again, nimbly and light-heartedly, unnoticed now, as they had all gone back to the hut without a further thought about the solitary climber. They could not see him and they could not help him – out of sight, out of mind.

I had now passed the main difficulties and had reached a slanting gully up which I sweated, first on the left wall and then on the right. Finally I went to the right, along a ledge to the crest of the ridge, and paused for breath. I stopped for a while on the summit, diverted for a time by an aircraft which passed rapidly by, leaving a long vapour trail in its wake.

I descended rapidly down the dark chimney and round the First Tower to the road. Whether the guardian was looking out of the window as I came down over the meadow, I do not know, but he was standing in the doorway and gave the impression that he had been waiting for the belated climber, myself, who had now resumed everyday life and only wanted to return home to prepare his lectures for the next day. I stood by my car, under the neon lights in place of the sunset; everybody had gone home, the parking lot was empty and the guardian, now that he saw that the man was neither hungry nor thirsty, shut the door and put out the light.

'Yes,' I said, going back to my desk, 'you've got to be lucky.'

'I don't understand that,' said one of the students as though I had not explained a mathematical problem very well.

'If you'd been up at the hut, I have no doubt that you would have asked some damn silly questions.'

The students laughed.

'After all it's really quite simple,' I said looking down at my hands which were scarcely grazed.

'Quite simple?'

'All I had to do was to let go.'

NANGA PARBAT 1970

It was about this time that I received the final invitation to join the Sigi-Low Memorial Expedition, which I accepted. Our objective was the 4500-metre South Face of Nanga Parbat, the highest rock and ice wall on earth.

This Rupal Flank had become one of the greatest unsolved mountain problems of the world and several unsuccessful attempts had been made on it. I had followed these attempts with close attention, had studied photographs of the face with care and I formed the conclusion that its difficulties were about equivalent to those met with on severe ascents in the Western Alps. Its height can be gauged from the following comparisons:

The Rupal Face is approximately two and a half times as high as the North Face of the Eiger, four times that of the North-West Face of the Civetta and eight times that of the Cima Grande. On top of this is its elevation above sea-level and its inaccessibility.

Based on my experiences in the Andes, I foresaw the extreme difficulties, the hazards and the physical exhaustion in the 'death zone' and I organised my training accordingly.

As I had to contribute a large sum of money towards participation in the expedition, I broke off my studies in Padua and took a job at the secondary school in Eppan, teaching mathematics, physics and physical culture. Most mornings I spent in the classrooms, but I devoted my afternoons to training.

I had worked out that every kilogram of surplus weight in climbing uses up calories and therefore oxygen, which is extremely deficient at heights of over 7000 metres above sea-level. I also realised that the legs have the hardest job to do, so I began to develop my thighs and calves rather than the muscles of my torso.

157

I therefore stopped climbing and went in for uphill running. I did a daily uphill run from Bolzano to Jenesien. I did this 1000 metres on my toes without a rest and it only took me less than an hour. Simultaneously I did breathing exercises and ate and drank at extended intervals in order to accustom my kidneys to extreme conditions.

In my opinion there are three stages of endurance: The first stage, which is attained by any healthy being, permits three or four hours of exertion without evoking any symptoms of fatigue, hunger or thirst.

The second stage, which has to do with the storing up of glycogen in the liver, I did not usually reach until after a few big climbs in the summer. During this phase of my training I was able to climb all day long without experiencing any hunger at midday and scarcely any thirst. My condition was about the same as after a night's bivouac and my capacity for concentration increased.

The third phase, which I never attained in the Alps, I only encountered on Nanga Parbat and in the jungles of New Guinea. On both these expeditions I was forced by unforeseen circumstances to continue climbing for several days under conditions of maximum exertion and without food or drink. In conditions like these one is much more dependent upon the capacity for exertion of the internal organs than upon a show of strength. Above all, the liver and kidneys must become acclimatised to extreme conditions of this nature.

When I commenced my training I had not reckoned on encountering such desperate conditions as those on Nanga Parbat, I had merely expected that they would be very much worse than normal and planned my training accordingly. Although I did not know the Himalayas, I realised that the hazards grew with increasing height. It is a fundamental rule that the difficulties and exertion met with must be superior to anything encountered in the Alps. This, however, demands many months of preparation. During the march in to the mountain one may get into one's stride, but the necessary preparation for the ascent of an 8000-metre peak must have been developed long before the start.

During the course of my many expeditions I have observed how completely untrained men have suffered bodily collapse on ascending to the first high-level camp or even on the way to base camp. They should obviously never be allowed anywhere near any hazard zones, as they might endanger the lives of their companions. Fat climbers are also a menace but a limited amount of overweight might perhaps not inhibit well-trained men at the start of a relatively easy ascent. I was prepared right from the start to meet with extreme conditions on the Rupal Face, so I watched my weight and kept it down to about 160 pounds.

I did not make any further changes in my diet. Normally I eat little meat, mainly carbohydrates and a lot of fruit. In order to be sure of a bowel movement, I instituted a day of fruit once a week and drank a lot of milk. I ate a lot of garlic before I set off for Nanga Parbat, as I had read that it increased the elasticity of the vascular walls.

I would like to stress emphatically that in my opinion it is important for anyone going on a great expedition to retain his normal eating habits, as any change can overload the organism.

I did not sleep any more than normal, usually about six or seven hours, and reserved at least four hours a day for training, thereby preserving a state of bodily well-being as though I had returned from a long vacation.

Over the Christmas holidays four of us attempted a winter ascent of the North Face of Monte Pelmo. Günther, who had been invited at the last moment to join the Nanga Parbat Expedition, and I were trying to reach the state of hardiness required for a great Himalayan expedition on this icy face. After bivouacking twice, we were surprised by a sudden storm and had to abseil off. The face became plastered with snow and we had to plough our way through masses of new snow back' to the car.

After a few months I really began to enjoy my training and I often did long periods of running. My morning cold showers had become a habit and even now I cannot do without them. I endeavoured to slow down my heart beats and increase the circulation in my hands and feet. Thanks to my long-distance running, my legs had developed at the expense of my trunk muscles and my pulse rate had gone down to forty-two a minute. I was very satisfied with the results of my training,

159

although I gave up climbing four months before I left for Nanga Parbat.

At the same time I had made an intensive study of photographs of the mountain and immersed myself in its literature, also talking to people who had been there. All this convinced me that it must be a sheer impossibility to climb the mountain by the Rupal Flank. When we left, doubts and certainty over the possibility of success were finely balanced. Our enthusiasm was great but I felt infinitely small when I came face to face with the mountain.

Six months later, Günther and I stood on the summit of Nanga Parbat. Owing to unforeseen circumstances, we were forced to descend by the easier West Face. We succeeded but Günther was carried away by an avalanche at the foot. I searched for him for a long time and then dragged myself with frozen feet down the Diamir Valley for days on end. We had been forced to traverse the 'naked mountain' unprepared and unplanned. For three days I was without drink and five without food, I spent three nights on the ice without shelter, finally I crawled down the valley as I could no longer stand on my feet.

Climbers all over the world said that it was a miracle that I had survived the ordeal but I do not believe in miracles.